Anglicanism: The Answer to Modernity

Anglicanism:
The Answer to Modernity

Edited by
Duncan Dormor, Jack McDonald
and Jeremy Caddick

continuum
LONDON • NEW YORK

Continuum

The Tower Building   370 Lexington Avenue
11 York Road   New York
London SE1 7NX   NY 10017-6503

www.continuumbooks.com

First published 2003

British Library Cataloguing-in-Publication Data
A catalogue record for this book is available
from the British Library.

ISBN 0-8264-6699-0

Typeset by Ray Davies
Printed and bound by
Creative Print and Design, Wales

Contents

Part III Engagement

Part IV Identity

Preface

The Most Reverend and Right Honourable
Dr Rowan Williams,
Archbishop of Canterbury

'The answer to insomnia is to read Williams's books.' 'The answer to global poverty is the overthrow of capitalism.' 'The answer to AIDS is chastity.' 'The answer to inefficiency is deregulation.' The title of this book might suggest that modernity is one of those easily recognizable problems to which someone ought to be able to find an easy solution; and there is a good deal here that could support such a reading. 'Modernity' is not seen in these pages as an unequivocally good or even a neutral thing, but as a complex net of attitudes and practices that leaves us stranded when it comes to making decisions requiring more than simple calculations of profit and effectiveness – whether in international affairs, sexual conduct or bioethics. Modernity is not a single system but an atmosphere in which people become increasingly *formless*, cut off from what could give their lives in any given present moment some kind of lasting intelligibility. Naturally enough, it is an atmosphere in which religious concern is hard for people to understand. Many of the traditional 'bridges' between religious discourse and daily concerns seem to have disappeared; the territory of cultural reference in which religious literacy can be taken for granted has shrunk dramatically. How are we to respond, we who continue to have religious, and in particular Christian, commitments?

In such context, so this book claims, Anglicanism has a good deal to offer. It may not have the cultural purchase it once enjoyed, but it still, in much of the United Kingdom assumes a responsibility for the local, accessible expression of religious concern. It is committed to performing its rites in every locality in the country, most of which rites are not well frequented, but some of which remain a point of resource for a majority in circumstances of stress, transition, loss and so on. There is a certain concern for simply allowing local communities to discover what God might be saying, without too much prescription about what they are permitted to hear.

But putting it this way already suggests that the initial way in which the title might be read could be misleading. Instead of a rather triumphalist proclamation that Anglican worship and theology are the solution to a particular problem, the actual ways in which Anglican practice works point to something different. Modernity is a set of questions, preoccupations and anxieties, and Anglicanism is equipped to engage with them in what one of our authors calls 'conversational' mode. Anglicanism 'answers' modernity because it has bothered to listen to it and thinks it worth talking with. In a good conversation, something is genuinely *contributed* towards a common future, but always in response to the reality of what's presented, rather than in lecturing or preaching mode. It is easy to pretend with some affection of superiority that this is a weak and unconfident style – and this has regularly been said about Anglicanism (and is said, in no friendly spirit, by some Anglicans themselves). But conversation in fact assumes quite a bit of confidence, since it requires a high degree of confidence to enter into an unstructured conversational exchange convinced that there will be opportunity for what you believe to emerge strongly enough to challenge and even transform whomever you are talking to.

These essays are not at all without confidence. They arise

from the experience of working with an agenda that has not been set by the Church, and yet trying within that both to serve and to subvert the dominant agenda in the name of God's gift and God's commonwealth. Some readers will be suspicious of a book written by deans and chaplains to an academic institution, on the grounds that universities, especially 'elite' universities, are isolated from the real preoccupations of the day. This is far from the truth. Apart from the fact that nearly all the contributors to this volume have professional training and experience outside academic theology (a very different situation from what might have prevailed in Cambridge chapels even half a generation ago), they are persuaded that the culture of young people in this environment obliges their pastors to engage more deeply than they would otherwise do with the major currents of modern assumptions about persons and values. They do not work in a protected atmosphere: rather the contrary.

So there is here a confidence about the theological task, a confidence about the categories of classical orthodox doctrine and ethics, and about the resources of Holy Scripture; and a confidence about the continuing ability of Anglicanism to engage with the hardest of contemporary issues and so to inform the mind of British society that it can be liberated from all that makes modernity a problem, from the shrinking of moral imagination that so frighteningly dehumanizes our decisions. There is no sense of a desire to take over, to impose solutions, to reverse history; but what is going to take 'history' forward, in a time of short-term thinking and functional or managerial solutions to difficulties, except a recovery of theological perspective – the categories of creation, wisdom, sin, covenant, incarnation, praise?

The contributions offered in this collection will not be uncontroversial. Some readers will look for more of a clarion call to sort out the tangles of legal establishment one way or the other;

many will question whether recognition of sustained cohabitation as a kind of covenant will do justice to what biblical and traditional ethics have sought to say about the right use of sexuality; the theodicy sketched here will provoke all the questions that theodicies invariably do. Some too will ask about whether a more Christocentric emphasis is needed for these reflections to do their full work. But none of these essays attempts to say the last word; only to suggest, as they all do with intelligence and originality, that the style of local, companionable presence and patient conversation that has been typical of Anglican reflections and witness has the capacity for some far more radical undermining of modernity's unreflective, impatient attitudes than might be expected. There is still a solid case to be made for an Anglican way that is content with a sacramental rather than an organizational and ideological unity, and with a mode of doing theology that is not too nervous of responding to questions that are actually being asked. The authors plead with the Anglican Church in these islands not to throw away the opportunities they have by focusing on the kind of housekeeping which conveys a painful unconcern with the realities of a profoundly needy and confused society. What Jesus Christ has to say to 'modernity' can all too easily be muffled by the Church's efforts to solve its problems before sharing its wisdom. It is an appeal that needs to be heard.

Notes on Contributors

JEREMY CADDICK has been Dean of Emmanuel College since 1994. He is a member of the Faculties of Biology and Divinity at the University of Cambridge and lectures on medical ethics to theologians and medical students. He previously served as a university chaplain in medical and veterinary schools in London and as a Priest Vicar of Westminster Abbey.

MAGGI DAWN was for a number of years a professional musician (guitar and bassist) and singer. She worked extensively in the field of contemporary religious music, writing new music for Christian festivals, cathedral and church liturgies, and 'Alternative Worship' projects. She has featured regularly on programmes by BBC Religion and Anglia TV, and has released five albums. In 1993 Maggi trained for the priesthood in Cambridge, where she also read for a PhD in theology and literature. She is now Chaplain to King's College, where she continues to write and teach modern theology. Previous publications include a chapter in *The Postevangelical Debate* (Cray et al, SPCK, 1997).

DUNCAN DORMOR is Dean of St John's College, Cambridge, and lectures in the Divinity Faculty on the sociology and anthropology of religion. A demographer by training, he worked for the charity ONE plus ONE, Marriage and Partnership Research, publishing on the topics of marriage, cohabitation and divorce, before being ordained to a curacy at St Peter's, Wolverhampton. He is currently finishing a book re-evaluating the practice of 'living together' from a Christian perspective to be published shortly, *Just Cohabiting?* (DLT, 2003).

TIMOTHY JENKINS is Dean and Fellow of Jesus College, and Assistant Director of Research in the Study of Religion in the Department of Theology and Religious Studies at Cambridge. A social anthropologist by training, who has undertaken fieldwork in France and England, he has recently published *Religion in English Everyday Life* (Berghahn Books, 1999).

JACK McDONALD was born and educated in Lancashire. After taking degrees in theology and philosophy, and teaching in a grammar school, he served as a curate in Camberwell before returning to Cambridge, where he is Dean of Gonville and Caius College and Senior Proctor of the University. In addition to researching into French Revolutionary deism, he sits on the Standing Advisory Council on RE for the County of Cambridgeshire and is Chair of Governors at a local primary school.

JEREMY MORRIS read Modern History at Balliol College, Oxford, where he also completed a doctorate on religion and social change. Later he read theology at Cambridge and trained for the ministry at Westcott House, where he returned, after a curacy in Battersea, as Director of Studies and then Vice-Principal. He is married, with three children. His research and teaching interests include modern Anglican history and theology, ecumenism, and ecclesiology. He is working on a book on the ecclesiology of F. D. Maurice. In 2001 he took up the position of Dean of Trinity Hall, Cambridge, where he is also Robert Runcie Fellow in Ecclesiastical History.

BEN QUASH is Dean of Peterhouse. He teaches Christian doctrine at Cambridge, with a particular interest in the nineteenth-century background to modern theology, twentieth-century Catholic and Protestant thought, philosophical theology, and Christian ethics. He was an undergraduate at Peterhouse

(1987–90), reading English, and then (as a second degree, while in training for ordination at Westcott House) theology. Doctoral work on the theological dramatic theory of Hans Urs von Balthasar (1905–88) combined these literary and theological interests. His book *Balthasar at the End of Modernity* (with Lucy Gardner, David Moss and Graham Ward) was published by T. & T. Clark in 1999, and *Following God: The Ethical Character of Christian Life* (a study course in Christian ethics) by STETS in 2000. He is currently completing a longer book on Balthasar's concept of 'Theodramatics' and the theology of history.

JO BAILEY WELLS is Lecturer in Old Testament and Biblical Theology at Ridley Hall in Cambridge. Dr Wells was previously Dean of Clare College, Cambridge, the first ordained woman to fulfil such a role. Among her other publications she is the author of *God's Holy People: A Theme in Biblical Theology* (Sheffield, 2000). She is currently working on a devotional commentary on Isaiah. She enjoys bringing the fruits of academic scholarship to pastoral effect in the Church, and to that end writes regularly for the Bible Reading Fellowship and the Scripture Union. She is also Moderator for the training of Readers in the Diocese of Ely. She is married to Sam, a parish priest and writer, and they have one son.

Introduction

Theology, Wisdom and the Future of the Church of England

*Duncan Dormor, Jack McDonald
and Jeremy Caddick*

Introduction

There is no disguising the fact that the Church of England could be in better shape. The figures of those attending its services are open to debate and massage, but for many the conclusion is inescapable: that a seemingly unstoppable decline is occurring. The most generous and optimistic polls place less than three million people in their parish churches for the folk festival of Christmas, and this in an English population of 49 million. This picture is reinforced by the demographic profile of active churchgoers. In a recent survey of the beliefs and practices of its readership conducted by the *Church Times*, respondents were categorized by age into four roughly equal groups: the 'young' (22 per cent) were categorized as those under 50.[1]

That said, parts of the Church of England, notably the Evangelicals, have experienced some growth in committed membership in recent years; and some pundits speak of a bottoming out of the decline, and even of the sniff of an upturn. But the Church cannot satisfy itself with news of modest expansion. The deceleration of shrinkage does not lessen the anxiety of the priest taking a christening that, however full the church, the theological diet of baptismal regeneration on offer is unlikely to merit the genuine assent of those present.

As a group of deans working in the University of Cambridge,

1

we feel that our position provides a helpful perspective on the future of the Church, where we see signs both positive and negative.

On the debit side, although we find ourselves working with and among people who are largely young, largely intelligent and largely moral, we find them to be largely uncomprehending of the mission and teaching which the Church of England, whether in college chapel or parish church, offers them. When they do think of their moral and spiritual development, the Church is not the first organization to which they turn.[2]

Some are resentful or afraid of a body they perceive as unwilling to enter into dialogue and still interested in stridently asserting its own version of the facts about the universe and of the true interpretation of those facts. There is a deeper dissonance between student expectations of dialogue, critical awareness and optimism, and the paternalistic dogmatism which they either see plainly in the Church, or sense is not far below the surface. What they yearn for is wisdom and to be good. What they are told by the Church to desire is to be saved and to be obedient.

However, the same set of circumstances can be read more hopefully. While it is true that fewer people come to our college chapels than a couple of generations ago, the communities thus formed are sincere, sustainable and vibrant. It has always been the case that the students who go to their university and college chapels will subsequently take their place in parish church and cathedral congregations. Given the age profile and promise of the communities we serve, the future for the Church as a whole is hopeful and interesting.

There are further and deeper reasons for confidence that the Church will continue to exercise a significant role. The accumulated wisdom of the Christian Church is rich and attractive fare indeed. Contrary to the popular received myths, we find that there is a curiosity and receptivity among our students for a Christian philosophy of life. Further, college communities are significant in that (for the time being) they manage to resist many of the pressures of social dislocation that are felt elsewhere. In these circumstances we find that there is a ready welcome for the ministry of a dean or a chaplain far beyond the boundaries of the community of committed believers. There is an understanding of the importance of such a role that feels tentatively for a religious approach to the world, while at the same time being repelled by dogmatism. We feel that the same is true at a national level, and that we can and should take advantage of the opportunities that the present time offers us. The Christian religion has many cultured admirers here, whose sympathies are alas dimmed by the Church of England's apparent determination to sell her intellectual, social and spiritual inheritance short.

That the Church of England should endeavour to operate on the broad canvas of the entire nation is axiomatic for us. Our particular ministry in a university underlines to us this breadth of ecclesiastical scope. The Church has long been intimately involved in all levels of national education, not merely as spectator and commentator but as instigator and shaper. Any relegation of this mainstream work to the periphery of the Church's concern we see as wholly misconceived. The Church of England's constitutional attachment to its primary and secondary schools and colleges of further education, and its traditional chaplaincy role in universities and elsewhere should compel the Church to function not as an arcane cultural ghetto but as a major player in the interpretation of developments in science, technology and the humanities, and in their implications for human life. Any vision narrower than this is a selling out of the future of English Christianity.

In seeking to address the ambiguous and uncertain situation

in which we find ourselves, we are emboldened by our double awareness of working in a Church of England which commands the active support only of one million people but which has a notional membership of 24 million, and of working in a university where, again, there are historic tolerances and sympathies for the Church of England but where the active and committed are few in number. In such a context, our desire is not primarily to increase the numbers of frequent worshippers in our chapels. Our larger desire is to transform this country for good in the light and wisdom of Christ.

We share this aim with the entire Church, of course. What gives our voice a particular accent is our existence as priests serving communities whose agendas are not supplied by the Church, but who rather require us to work to their agenda, in our case an academic one. We also note that the future leadership of the country, as well as of the Church, is to be found in university communities like ours. Our basic task is to provide an experience of the Church in which students can believe. Our method is to seek a Church which reflects the sort of ministry in which we are engaged. If this appears arrogant, it is only superficially so. It is inherent in our task as ministers of the Christian religion in a university that we cannot be arrogant – we are engaged in a university's agenda, not our own, and we could not hope to impose our language, mores and theology onto such a community, even should we wish it.

The future of the Church in Western civilization is likely to be along these minority lines. We are here to influence, to suggest, to debate, to accept, to challenge, and to point to a reality which transcends the worldly and which gives meaning and social, emotional and metaphysical shape to our experience. The future of the portion of Western civilization which is England is up for grabs. To our mind, Anglicanism should be at the very forefront of developing the exciting and commanding ideas which will form and improve that civilization.

The Background to this Volume

The spirit of Anglican thinking over the last century or so has often been expressed most effectively by the collaborative volume, a process initiated by the publication of *Essays and Reviews* in 1860.[3]

Some readers may be tempted to make particular comparisons between this book and another collection of essays published in Cambridge in 1962, *Soundings*. This is a natural comparison in at least two regards: first, some of the essays in the two volumes are written by people who hold the same post, and second, while some of the contributors to *Soundings* were venerable figures, most of them were young (of the '22 per cent'). While we acknowledge these superficial similarities, we insist that this is no *Soundings II*. This volume is concerned with advocating an inclusive and robust Christianity which finds a clear shape within Anglicanism.

This is not so much a work of theology as one of apologetic. Where *Soundings* intended to court controversy and open up a doctrinal debate, as *Essays and Reviews* had in 1860, this volume seeks to draw people to affirm the Anglican tradition critically and constructively. It is intended to be practical, rooted as it is in our particular pastoral context of work with students (see especially Jo Bailey Wells's chapter), but written by people who are profoundly concerned with parish life – which is, after all, where our congregations come from and go to. We do not intend to provide a radical review and intellectual restatement of faith, or as *Soundings* put it, 'to start all over again'. Rather, we perceive the need to commend the enduring efficacy of the Anglican way of being faithful to Christ.

Because of this desire, this is categorically not a party book. Its contributors are drawn from backgrounds and theological colleges which might be firmly located within the Evangelical, Catholic and Liberal parties of the Church. We, however, eschew the 'schismatic mind-set which has a nasty tendency to become an ecclesial habit' (p. 45) as pointless, introverted indulgence. Our agenda is simply the advocacy of the robust and inclusive form of Christianity conducive to human flourishing that we find in Anglicanism. There will be those who will in consequence perceive this to be a 'liberal' book; and while we would not wish to dismiss this term, we would qualify it: ours is an orthodox liberalism which takes Scripture and the tradition of Anglicanism and its resources very seriously.

Perhaps the most profound gulf between us and our predecessors concerns tone and context. *Soundings* struck a cautionary and prophetic note against a backdrop of the authority and assurance of the Church of England. Its publication marks a pivotal point in any account of post-war Anglicanism. The 1950s had been a time of religious consolidation, even of expansion, both in Britain and in many Western countries. Indeed, Grace Davie goes so far as to argue that the 1950s was a thoroughly Anglican decade in which the Church played a significant confirmatory role. It was in tune with the prevailing culture, never more so than at the Coronation of Elizabeth II in 1953.[4]

However, by 1962 it was clear that radical change was afoot. The mental dam of post-war austerity, of respectability and restraint was beginning to show clear cracks. *Soundings* was published in November, one month after the Beatles released 'Love me do' and in the same month that the biting iconoclastic satire of *That Was the Week that Was* was launched. In the following year 'sex was invented', and radical secularizing change gathered pace. As one social historian has put it, 'quite suddenly in 1963, something very profound ruptured the character of the nation and its people, sending organised Christianity on a downward spiral to the margins of social significance'.[5]

The statistics confirm this perception. While many indicators of religious adherence begin to fall in 1958, by 1963 such a fall was precipitous. Consider the most basic indicator of Church membership, baptisms. For every 1000 English children born in 1956, 602 were baptized – a figure very close to what had been occurring in the last years of Queen Victoria's reign (it had been 609 baptisms per 1,000 births in 1900). But by 1970 this figure had fallen dramatically to 466; and by 1999, the figure was 211. Confirmation figures indicate a similar decline. Some 190,713 people were confirmed in England in 1960. By 1970, this had almost halved to 113,005.[6] Similar figures could be quoted for a range of indicators of religious participation.

Half of the contributors to this volume were born after the publication of *Soundings*, and all have been formed by a culture in which Christianity has not been the dominant cultural player in England. We are therefore believers against the grain. That the Church of England is considered irrelevant by many is not news for us. At our remove from the 1960s, it shocks us neither intellectually nor emotionally.

This volume emerges not from a sense of foreboding of what lies ahead. It is genuinely unclear whether the decline of institutional allegiance and orthodox Christian belief will continue; it is by no means inevitable. Whatever the trends, however, we write because we believe. We believe that Anglicanism happens to provide the right type of answer to difficult questions faced by many people today; and that this answer is not abstract, but embodied, contextual and personal – and it works.

We are all ordained ministers, but we have all earned our way in the world before (as rock musician, teacher, press officer, administrator, and so on) and could do so again if necessary. We have no need to be defensive of the Church of England, because the Church does not pay our wages. We write then because we happen to believe in the Anglican way.

Presence, Inquiry, Engagement and Identity

There are several recurring emphases within this volume. One of these is a focus upon the role of Anglican faith in everyday experience, whether in pastoral ministry with students (Wells) or a parish context (Quash) or the Church's involvement through its attention to suffering (McDonald) or relationships (Dormor). Another is an attempt to broker understanding and bridge the gaps that can exist between the Church and the Academy (Dawn) or between Church and State (Morris) or more profoundly between the sacred and the secular (Jenkins, Caddick and Wells). However, we have found four themes – presence, inquiry, engagement and identity – to be particularly pertinent in our consideration of how Anglicanism might constitute an answer to the problems of modernity (by which we seek to include those aspects of it that some choose to label 'postmodern' or 'late modern').

Our first theme, in Part I, that of *presence*, finds its strongest resonances in the contributions of Jo Bailey Wells and Ben Quash. 'Where do bright young adults, finding their way and exploring life's possibilities, fit into the institution of the Church?' (p. 17). This is a question that many working in higher educational chaplaincy wrestle with on a daily basis. Wells's honest response in Chapter 1, 'at best awkwardly', takes her into an exploration of the wisdom literature of the Old Testament. Drawing on her own pastoral practice, she offers an 'applied apologetic' for ministry with young people. In an insightful account of what it means to be present to students as a pastor and mentor, Wells shows how the category of wisdom can be useful in bridging the secular and the sacred – over such everyday matters as money, conversation, friendship and work. Thus it serves for building up the common life of a community, providing 'some ancient insights for a postmodern context, and an effective, if unusual, path to faith' (p. 18). Drawing on the insights of Bonhoeffer and Rahner, Ben Quash in Chapter 2 outlines the human calling as one of being 'present to ourselves and to one other' (p. 38). Advocating a candid approach to living which involves the recognition and acknowledgement of others and an opposition to all manifestations of 'one-way looking', Quash explores his theme through a consideration of the 'embodied, contextual and personal' knowledge that forms part of the identity of the Church of England and the Anglican Communion. At the local level, Quash argues, the parish priest 'is often in the very privileged position of being able to describe what the truth of everyday life is in a particular locality', and that this is a 'a high and precious form of knowledge denied to outside observers, commentators and statisticians' (p. 47-8). At the global level he points to the extraordinary contextual knowledge of world events embodied in worldwide Anglicanism 'because of the way its presence to localities across the world is gathered up and shared at Communion level'. Commending the 'honest speaking and generosity and seriousness' (p. 45) manifest at the Primates' Meeting in Portugal in 2000, in the face of profound difference and the threat of schism, Quash concludes with a challenging call to unity: 'If we cannot shape a Church in which people are genuinely present to each other, we have nothing to offer the world. If we can shape such a Church, we make the trinitarian life itself manifest in our midst' (p. 56).

In Part II the second theme is that of *inquiry*. Here, Maggi Dawn and Jack McDonald explore the twin aspects of revelation and reason.

In Chapter 3 Maggi Dawn brings us to the thorny question of hermeneutics as she seeks to address potential divisions between Academy and Church over the way they handle texts in order that the Christian faith, dependent on the Bible as its foundation, can embrace new developments without sacrificing the integrity of faith. Drawing for inspiration on the example of Samuel Taylor Coleridge whose seminal writing on the subject was coincident with the rise of modern critical approaches to the Bible, she argues that the future of Christian hermeneutics depends on us grasping the point that text is a means of voicing the living truth of Christ, not of preserving a historical and dying religion.

The Church of England is perceived by some to be obsessed with comparatively trivial issues. This observation is the starting point for Jack McDonald's return in Chapter 4 to a very old question, the mystery of evil, 'the very mention of [which] injects welcome seriousness into the debate which the theist can have with the materialist' (p. 83). As the Church is attentive to 'the grinding business of living and coping with the reality of evil-suffered and evil-done' (p. 83), that is, through its conduct of funerals and through its work in hospital and hospice chaplaincy, it possesses unique experience and credibility when it turns to consider the intellectual question of the Problem of Evil. McDonald considers this in conversation with what he describes as the 'Pessimistic metaphysics', characteristic of those who slavishly follow an Augustinian understanding of the Fall, and a more optimistic account exemplified by the work of the Lutheran philosopher, G. W. Leibniz. While not uncritical of the latter's approach, McDonald roots his account firmly in universal reason rather than particular revelation, and thereby sees himself potentially alongside fellow theists from the Jewish and Muslim communities on a shared platform. The fundamental issue, he argues 'is the meaning and purpose of human existence in the light of our suffering, and not the future of any particular cultural manifestation of the religious impulse' (p. 103). Against the 'explanatory limitations and personal unimaginativeness of materialism' (p. 104), Active Optimism, he suggests, is the Anglican way *par excellence*.

Chapters 5 and 6 in Part III focus more explicitly on the *engagement* of the Church with the world. Here, Jeremy Caddick and Duncan Dormor address contemporary ethical issues; respectively, decisions relating to life and death and to love and marriage. While both are robust in their criticism of aspects of contemporary society, not least its relentless focus upon the individual as autonomous agent rather than as a person within the community, they also argue that the Church has taken its 'eye off the ball' (p. 122) and been concerned with addressing superficial issues.

The world of healthcare needs the traditional ethical wisdom embodied in Christianity, argues Caddick, in his consideration of the limitations of a rights-based approach to ethical decision-making. This assertion is approached through an exploration of the appeal made by Diane Pretty to a 'right to die', and the attempts of Natalie Evans and Lorraine Hadley to have the provisions of the Human Fertilization and Embryology Act set aside and to prevent the destruction of embryos, through an appeal to Human Rights legislation. Caddick argues that 'the framework of rights is, by itself, too insubstantial to guide us' (p. 112). Indeed, in a cogent attack upon on reproductive libertarianism, he comments on 'the wholesale inappropriateness of trying to say anything very meaningful about families and family relationships in terms of rights, autonomy and choice' since 'the single most important feature of family relationships is that they *do not* rest on choice' (p. 119). He then seeks to demonstrate how in all these cases, whether it is acknowledged or not, 'the debate can be seen to draw on the richer ("thicker" or more culturally conditioned) resources that are on offer in the Christian tradition' (p. 126).

Duncan Dormor's call for the Church to reconsider its approach to pre-nuptial cohabitation is founded upon a belief that the innovation of modern contraception is a Promethean step, the full sociological implications of which the Church has not fully appreciated. Taking issue with contemporary sociological accounts of modern relationships, in which 'the sexual and emotional dimensions of the relationship are ... subservient to the rationality of utilitarian calculus, and the individual is conceived to be, in the heart of their identity ... a consumer' (p. 144), Dormor challenges the Church to look again at the practice of cohabitation. He argues that cohabitation is now 'an integral part of couple formation' which blurs 'the previous clear-cut distinctions between "going steady", engagement and the early years of marriage' (p. 146), but which does not constitute a rejection by young adults of the ideal of marriage. Furthermore, he suggests the Church has a crucial role in assisting couples to celebrate and confirm their loving in the commitment of marriage that speaks of the transcendent dimension of the human pairbond, and which also provides a framework for human living.

Finally, in Part IV, we turn to the central theme of *identity*, and to a consideration by Jeremy Morris of the Anglican Church as an Established Church, and to Tim Jenkins' controversial (but also ironic) assertion, echoed in the title of the book, that Anglicanism is the only answer to modernity.

In Chapter 7, through a careful survey of the history of the relationship between Church and State, Morris argues that the development of the modern State has proceeded on deliberately secular lines, and that arguments about Establishment must take account of that salient fact. In the company of other commentators, he makes a clear distinction between the national and

12

privileged (House of Lords, the monarchy) and the local and grounded (marriages, funerals, Church schools) dimensions of Establishment. Pleading for an end to the game of double-bluff on the part of the Church when it comes to this vexed question, he makes a 'qualified and conditional defence' of the existing relationship between Church and State, which has more force at the local level.

In perhaps the most ambitious chapter in the collection, Chapter 8, Jenkins brings an anthropologist's eye to the question of polity. He argues that to understand the Church of England, as with any institution, one must 'grasp the question to which it is a response' (p. 186). Anglicanism, he suggests, 'is a facing up of the Christian faith to the failure of religion' (p. 192) that lies at the heart of modernity. As a consequence, it is 'at least capable of holding in tension the antinomies of the modern condition' (p. 197). The point, then, of Establishment is that it is 'a functional way of continually drawing attention to the need on the part of all responsible people to contest idolatry' (p. 192). The strength and uniqueness of Anglicanism lie in its twin commitments to territorial embeddedness (the parish system) and a conversational (unexclusivist) mode, through which the Church can 'be used to think with' by others engaged in the exercise of fostering human flourishing. The Anglican settlement, for Jenkins, offers the country the 'possibility of charity, redemption and hope' which are 'frequently denied' in the secular realm – which tends towards 'calculation, repression and illusion'.

Coda

Clearly, this volume in its central assertion seeks to commend a particular manifestation of Christian faith as being especially well suited to crafting solutions to the pressing problems of our modern world. We expect others to be as loyal to their own traditions and, like us, to strive to be imaginative in their interpretation of them. Within our claim there is a straightforward intention to be both robust and inclusive. However, in a Europe increasingly marked by nominal belief, it would be ridiculous for Christians to be partisan and shrill in their denominational allegiance. We believe the Anglican Church has a discernible vocation in our pluralist context, but this is not a claim which is deaf to the claims of others. Indeed, we would welcome as partners in dialogue those from elsewhere within the Christian fold or those of other faith traditions.

Notes

1 Francis (2002). The Survey highlights profound differences between generations in matters of belief.
2 'The Church is seen as a welcoming place for the middle-aged and elderly: 85 per cent of respondents saw it as attractive to retired people, and 66 per cent to middle-aged people. But the percentage dropped severely for children (35 per cent), young adults (20 per cent), and teenagers (11 per cent)', Handley (2002), p. 1.
3 The process continued through *Lux Mundi* (1889), *Foundations* (1912), *Essays Catholic and Critical* (1926), *Soundings* (1962) and *Christ, Faith and History* (1972), to name the best known.
4 Davie (1994), p. 31.
5 Brown (2001), p. 1.
6 Figures quoted by Brown (2001), pp. 6–7, 191.

References

Brown, C. (2001) *The Death of Christian Britain*. London: Routledge.
Davie, G. (1994) *Religion in Britain since 1945*. Oxford: Blackwell.
Francis, L. (2002) 'Three visions of Christianity: Leslie Francis introduces the *Church Times* Survey', *Church Times*, 25 January, pp. 1–2.
Handley, P. (2002) 'Survey reveals sharp church age divide', *Church Times*, 25 January, p. 1.

Part I

Presence

1

Ancient and Postmodern:
Lessons from Wisdom for Ministry

Jo Bailey Wells

Introduction

Where might the book of Ecclesiastes fit into a structured biblical theology? Where do bright young adults, finding their way and exploring life's possibilities, fit into the institution of the Church? The answers are often similar. At best, they fit awkwardly; at worst, they do not find a place. Either they are forced uncomfortably into some prior categories; or a new, unsatisfactory, category is created specially for them.

I have come to rejoice in the broad and imprecise category of 'Wisdom' in the Old Testament.[1] It is ill-fitting: in Old Testament studies in general it refers to that literature which stands outside the primary flow of both historical narrative and law. There are three 'wisdom books' in the Old Testament: Proverbs, Job and Ecclesiastes.[2]

In this chapter I shall explore some of the contrasting and complementary aspects of faith that I see demonstrated within the wisdom tradition. These are aspects that I have found useful for understanding and interpreting the contemporary Christian life of faith – and in particular the ministry of a priest – in one particular corner of God's kingdom, a Cambridge College. Some of the insights gleaned from the wisdom literature have, for me, endorsed and enabled certain forms of ministry and expression that might otherwise seem marginal or alien to the Church. While many may know of the suffering of Job, few 'insiders' realize that Ecclesiastes fosters cynicism and hedonism, or that Proverbs teases and provokes.

And these are just the sort of themes that I have found effective in engaging students. Many would never begin by claiming interest in 'faith' in any conventional sense – certainly not to a priest! But in the wisdom books there are none of the 'code words' commonly associated with biblical faith – covenant, commandment, cult, tradition – certainly nothing normally regarded as givens within Jewish or Christian circles. It is in its very nature as ill-fitting that lies its appeal to a group of people who do not see their identity within an established system.

In the wisdom books we find 'a form of faith that is open to the world, that eschews authoritarianism, that has no interest in guilt, but that believes that life in God's world is a way of faith to be celebrated'.[3] It is not surprising that for some who have been numbed – or even wounded – by conventional forms of authoritarian faith, the teaching of wisdom is found to be an adequate alternative way to responsible life and joyful communion with God. As I shall illustrate by explanation and example, this was my experience at Clare College: wisdom offers some ancient insights for a postmodern context, and an effective, if unusual, path to faith.

Conformity and Challenge

The Book of Proverbs is the definitive wisdom teaching in the Old Testament. In its final form, the book is a rich collection of sayings that range from practical common-sense advice to cryptic assertions about the mysteries of existence. To some biblical interpreters these two extremes are irreconcilable. More recently they have been appreciated for the subtle and multiform way in which – together – they speak of God and his world.[4] The sayings are presented in the context of a family or community in which the older members are socializing the young into a set of attitudes and behaviours. 'This is how life is,' they say, 'and this is how we live it.'

Such material may not at first appear promising for today's students, whom I have found to be acutely sensitive to anything patronizing, matronizing or prescribed. But the teaching is not heavy and 'directive'. Through various rhetorical strategies the hearer is invited to complete the connection, to reason out something that is implied.[5] Thus the teaching is offered without heavy authoritarian insistence; rather, the proverbs serve as invitations to reflection, in which the listener is expected to make connections toward which only hints are supplied. Even in the longer speeches where a theology is more fully developed, it is the artistry that carries the authority. Wisdom teachers do not announce 'Thus says the LORD,' like the prophets.

It has been common among biblical scholars of the modern era to view Israel's wisdom as 'secular', not least because – on the face of it – the sayings relate to activity in the world that makes little direct reference to God. Moreover, some of the material appears to draw on texts from other parts of the Ancient Near East. Yet, the very celebration of creation itself is a celebration of the Creator. In Proverbs, underlying the metaphors of the two ways, the two houses and the two women, is an understanding of creation as ordered by God. Finding wisdom means discovering how to follow the order that God has built into his world. This is what a later era would describe as subscribing to natural law, or following 'the grain of the universe'.[6]

Furthermore, the wisdom literature holds creation and redemption closely together. Proverbs, Job and Ecclesiastes all assert that the fear of *the LORD* (YHWH) is the beginning of wisdom.[7] Here the validity of the historical and prophetic traditions of Israel is assumed. Yahweh is the name of Israel's redeemer God who rescued the nation from slavery in Egypt and brought them to himself.[8] Thus, from a canonical perspective, this material – secular though it may appear – does not eschew Israelite tradition; it depends upon it and meanwhile even embraces (to some degree) the traditions of others.

Contemporary culture has an uneasy relationship with tradition. If modernity rejected it, in the hope that reason would lead to new truths, then postmodernity has questioned the limitless power of reason. Amidst the undermining of old certainties is a hunger for ancient traditions – and a longing to know how to make sense of their plurality.

The wisdom literature of the Bible offers one model. Here wisdom sayings of several traditions and cultures are valued. They are brought together generously, within a single framework. Because the fabric of creation comes from God, wisdom may be found and is to be sought in every area of human life. There is no need for defensive critique or forceful assertion concerning the wisdom of 'foreigners' – for God is the 'given', the source of all nations and all being, who stands as the overarching meta-narrative which surrounds all human narratives.[9] There is a freedom in plurality because of the stability, the security, which lies behind everything. Diversity can be celebrated because – ultimately – it exists in harmony. There is the confidence of unity, under God.

In the work of a College Dean I recognize certain parallels involving diversity, security and freedom. At the beginning of a new academic year it is common for new students to ask, 'What is the work of a Dean?' Perhaps the title conjures up images of an eccentric academic imposing some outdated values, or an ageing cleric in lonely devotion; whereas I, in my effort to look young and lively, am unnerving. 'To make the workings of the college human and its worship divine', has been my favourite answer. Sometimes this response disturbed certain assumptions or stereotypes. It bridges the secular and the sacred; it focuses the multi-faceted character of a community; it unites past and present.

Whether by divine design or historic accident, such ministry is supported by the establishment but not limited by its boundaries. As with the extraordinary achievement of Old Testament wisdom, it depends upon the weight of tradition yet is free to sit lightly, embracing those who may not wish to acknowledge it, responding to the riches beyond it, and above all, taking risks. Deans (or Chaplains) can thus be radical yet conservative; they can innovate yet be faithful; they can fully serve a 'secular' institution (as well as members of different faith traditions within it), even while functioning as Christian priests.

We have discussed the teaching of Proverbs – subtle, accessible yet nevertheless didactic in sustaining suggestions and guidance for living life well. The other two wisdom books complement these norms but in a rather different way. Job and Ecclesiastes have been termed variously as reflective wisdom or questioning wisdom. They react to the 'givens' established in Proverbs with probing challenges. As well as suggesting that 'This is how life is and this is how we live it', the wisdom literature is not afraid to respond in critique, 'We tried it, but it didn't work.'

So also with the pastoral aspects of a Dean's ministry. A Dean is one who can stand on the sidelines with the perspective and the authority to critique a college system. Their loyalty is total but it is not an unquestioning loyalty; it does not preclude challenge, where this is relevant or appropriate. Moreover they have a higher loyalty; their life or 'career' does not depend on the college. Likewise, a Dean is not unaware of those who encounter the darker side of life, of those for whom the logic of Proverbs does not work.

Experience

Wisdom literature is a reflection upon lived experience of quite mundane kinds. It suggests a model for finding meaning even in the daily grind. Proverbs directs attention to the ways of an ant (Proverbs 6:6), to controlling the temper (Proverbs 19:19), to food and drink (Proverbs 20:1; 23:20f.). Whereas 'historical faith' tends to focus on great public crisis and transformations (like the Exodus, the Entry into the land, and the Exile), wisdom focuses on the daily routines of human interaction. It begs questions about the meaning of everyday matters such as money, conversation, friendship and work. It takes such things with great seriousness and recognizes that the right use and enjoyment of these daily realities are the real stuff of human life. Only through this piecemeal engagement with the experiences and details of life in a community over time, are the processes of the social world accumulated and communicated.[10]

Here is inspiration for the hours of loitering and listening that befall a pastor immersed in the life of a community. With this in view I was renewed in my intention to maintain an open door and the time for conversation even when what is urgent threatens to appear more important. I saw the value of time spent with an individual: even just for offering the simple encouragement that helped keep someone going, or the sounding board that provided a sense of perspective. The very details of an individual's worries, or a couple's communication, or a family's dysfunction, are precisely the material from which life is better understood and thus wisdom is gained – the kind of wisdom one might call 'common sense' with the benefit of hindsight. 'The shape of living' is discerned not in large doses but one item at a time.[11]

This work is aptly termed mentoring. It is a classical model, not unlike the teacher–disciple relationship. In both sacred and secular realms, it currently enjoys a resurgence of popularity. Whereas traditional Western models of learning have been didactic – learning through lectures, for example – this model underlines the learning from experience, through developing the art of reflection. It becomes the goal of such reflection to develop a way of distinguishing the significant from the trivial, of seeing the extraordinary in the ordinary, to seek the path of wisdom even among the habits that might otherwise be described as boring. It is to discern 'how, in the midst of an overwhelming world, our lives can be shaped'.[12]

This feature of the wisdom literature is particularly striking in a place like Cambridge. A university is necessarily a place where students gather to learn from experts: thus, where conventional, conservative models of teaching and learning predominate. In a climate where wisdom is presumed to be found in libraries, a declaration of the wisdom that may be gleaned from one's own experience is radical and essential even if – as with the wisdom literature within the Old Testament as a whole – it remains marginal. Experience is not the whole story, but it is valid.

Even within so-called 'enlightened' institutions of learning – those that recognize A.P.E.[13] for example – the wisdom reflections of the Old Testament present a challenge. For this literature embraces experience that might itself be considered marginal. The Book of Proverbs develops its own theodicy, whereby God's goodness and justice are defended even when there is suffering and injustice in the world. That is, Proverbs does not ignore poverty or tragedy, even while it attempts an explanation of the elusive ways of God.

As every mentor knows, however, the rawness and raggedness of lived experience do not uniformly adhere to any patterns; it is at this point that any simple theodicy is challenged. Such protest is the stuff of Ecclesiastes and Job, but especially Job.

With theatrical fervour, Job enters into dispute with God and with his 'friends', rejecting all conventional accounts of reality and inviting the audience to rethink its settled convictions. Driven by 'unacceptable' experiences, Job offers a model for re-evaluating the givens and reopening life with God to question and wonder and risk. The concerns with which Job tackles God receive their response not in reasoned explanation or didactic truth. Indeed, it is often noted that he does not receive any answers to his questions. Rather, through an experience of God, Job's questions are outnarrated.

Ethical Direction

The Book of Proverbs is presented as 'instruction in wise dealing ... Knowledge and prudence to the young' (Proverbs 1:3–4). Through both wise sayings ('proverbs') and through direct, mostly negative, instructions ('you shall not ...'), guidance is offered as to how to live well. This is ethics. Yet, whereas quotations from Genesis or Leviticus are commonplace along-side the gospels and Paul when the Bible is quoted in contemporary ethical debate, it is rare to see reference to the wisdom literature. There are two reasons why the contribution of the wisdom books to ethics has been overlooked or ignored.

First, rather than being specific to Israelite – or Judaeo-Christian – tradition, the ethic is presented as having universal application. The sayings seem to arise from folklore and appear as the trusted, time-tested aphorisms of a family or community, *any* family or community. They provide an entire social code for acceptable attitudes and behaviour universally.

The direct prohibitions – for example, 'do not remove an ancient landmark' (Proverbs 23:10) – are generally asserted without explanation or sanction, as if they were universally accepted. Indeed, the section in Proverbs 17:22–24:22 bears close resemblance to the Egyptian wisdom of Amenemope: this wisdom is not uniquely asserted in Israel. There are few specifically Yahwistic elements throughout.[14] Rather, we find a system of cause and effect that might be attached to the hard-working deserving middle class anywhere, akin to 'work hard at school so that you get a good job afterwards'. Such logic falls comfortably into the secular middle-class environment of a college, therefore, but does not appeal readily to those seeking to identify a distinctive biblical ethic.

Second, the wisdom literature demonstrates an approach to ethics that runs counter to the crisis moments of decision-making. Wisdom ethics is not so much geared to the dilemmas and decisions *in extremis* – as in the popular ethical debates that arise over a particular IVF case, or genetic breakthrough, or terrorist threat, for example. It is, more fundamentally, focused on the normal habits of life, those things that are more usually taken for granted.[15] The wisdom literature recognizes the ethical significance of these everyday details. Wise living consists in (1) respecting the 'givens' of daily life; (2) making responsible choices about those things that are negotiable; and (3) anticipating the consequences of those choices. The Book of Proverbs in particular develops ethical notions of cause and effect; more specifically of 'character and consequence',[16] i.e. that living wisely – choosing the way of wisdom rather than folly – leads to blessing.

Nevertheless, it is usually a moment of crisis that prompts a person to seek pastoral help and spend time in reflection. An enduring role of the minister working within a college community – a community where people know each other at least by name – is to listen to those facing decisions and support them through that process. The model of wisdom is invaluable here: it has been my practice to help a person establish the givens of a situation (1) and the hopes for the future (3) in order to address the needful choices in the present (2). This carries a person beyond the present uncertainties to future goals, from which they can work backwards. Sometimes the necessary action then becomes obvious. I have found the simple question, 'What sort of a person do you want to be?' to be the strategic one: this is, essentially, a paraphrase from wisdom; and it is worked out through the experiment of life, through reflection on experience.

Further to this practice, I have encouraged a person to ponder 'What is the best thing that could happen?' and 'What is the worst thing that could happen?' It is, of course, helpful to name the fears – after which, they characteristically diminish in proportion. Here again, the wisdom literature offers the model: indeed, in the story of Job, it describes the worst in terms of vivid and terrifying experience; and yet all is not finally lost, if faith persists.

Job and Ecclesiastes testify to the possibility that the worst thing *can* happen. Job is said to be 'blameless and upright' (Job 1:1, 8; 2:3) and thus, according to the conventional wisdom theodicy recounted in Proverbs, he is a prime candidate deserving of 'peace and prosperity' (cf. Psalms. 25:21; 37:37). But the worst *does* happen, and the Book of Job discredits all conventional ethical explanations, as suggested by Job's wife (2:9). In this situation the pastor must take heed how *not* to counsel: although Job's friends try to be helpful by reminding Job of some major theological truths, they are counter-productive and hurtful. They are an example of how good and godly people who have the best of intentions can nevertheless say things that are untrue, because they push partial truths too far. Indeed, the book underlines the importance of the pastoral role to the 'friends': to take responsibility for guiding the community in which 'Job' lives and suffers, helping others to respond appropriately and cope personally.

Conversation

We have suggested that the wisdom books consist of reflection based on experience. We might therefore imagine an inventory of memories and anecdotes that have been compiled to impart advice – perhaps of the sort that begins, 'When I was young ...' (at which anyone present who *is* young yawns). But no; wisdom is communicated through speech. We find reflections and interpretations of experience that are crafted into compelling and persuasive rhetoric. Even when it is read from the pages of a book, it speaks with a dramatic voice and can be heard, as if with the ears. Though directed to the young ('My son, ...'), it communicates in relatively non-hierarchical ways: the tone is that of an older person sharing with a younger person what they wish they'd understood earlier in life. It is done with humour and playfulness, using images, metaphors and figures of speech.

The material does not appear systematized; indeed, generations of scholars have despaired of understanding Proverbs or Ecclesiastes in their final form, and have preferred a fragmentary approach that rearranges the material into thematic categories or possible historical strands. But speech is seldom flatly ordered or systematic: this speech, at least, appears *ad hoc*, taking on a typically postmodern 'pastiche' character. And the Proverbs text records many different voices anyway. The conversational art depends on some mystery: leaving listeners to make connections and do some puzzle-solving for themselves.[17]

The activity of speech invites conversation and response. It thus counters individualism; it both presumes and enables community in which there is sharing and persuading and debate. Such mutual learning is just the kind of activity for which Oxbridge Colleges were designed. Even the architecture of the colleges is intended to foster community and conversation and learning between people of different stages and subjects of study.[18] Members live on staircases with shared facilities – forming interdisciplinary 'family' groups – which are arranged around a court or quad, where there is the space for a distance of respect ('do not walk on the grass').

I recall spending many long evenings as a student myself deep in conversation and discussion on the matters of the day, whether sacred or secular. I confess to having been disappointed with this aspect in my exposure to student life more recently: a hesitancy to engage in debate. I find this is as true of social and political as of theological matters. If this is indeed a fading habit, I do not believe it can be attributed to complacency. Perhaps it is a feature of a multi-faith world of choice – 'whatever you believe is fine for you but leave me alone' – but such attitudes speak to me of protectionism as much as pluralism. That is, I will act to protect myself from exposure or pain or challenge because I am lonely and vulnerable and disillusioned. The archetypal postmodern student feels disconnected and longs for community – a place to belong – but fears the radical engagement this may involve.

It has been a habit for many years at Clare that those who come to preach in the Chapel – usually each Sunday at Evensong – stay not only for a meal with the congregation but for coffee and discussion afterwards. Having listened to the rhetoric of a sermon, members of the congregation are given the right of reply. But how much more readily have those who dislike or disagree with a sermon simply slipped away, unobtrusively if not invisibly. So often it is preferable to walk out rather than to challenge the speaker, to slip away rather than articulate an argument. There is fear of offence; there is fear of exposure. Am I still welcome if I want to challenge their premises? Does God *exist*? Is this a world made up of people and forces I can trust? Can I even formulate the questions I am asking? Should I bother? Are there any givens?

One of the tasks that I have understood to fall within the role of Dean is to foster the kind of community that counters detachment and loneliness and that enables honest, safe, meaningful, face-to-face conversation (e-mail is not enough!), in both formal and informal ways. At times I have used a carefully articulated question to initiate engagement and break the ice.[19] All of the time, the process involves guarding the safe space – I think of the rectangle of grass in the court – that allows for discovery and growth and change.[20] In such circumstances, the college can imitate the pattern of wisdom, whereby the shape of living is suggested and explored mutually, and all can find themselves both teachers and learners on the path.

This kind of community eschews the boundaries of 'the sacred' and 'the secular' just as wisdom does. Theological debate is by no means limited to those who study theology, any more than political debate is confined to those who study politics. The experience of living involves the sacred and the secular – just as Clare College Old Court encompasses a Chapel and a Hall and some Common Rooms and a bar. A holistic search to establish the shape of living will include all these realms. As far as possible, I have refused the sort of labels that might otherwise be attached to 'Chapel-goers' or 'religious types', so as to allow for the subliminal space where people may lurk – to attend Chapel occasionally without being collared – and where change is more possible and more comfortable. This is not to blur the real distinctions between people who are different – specifically between those who call themselves 'Christians' and those who do not. Rather, it is to permit people to inhabit grey areas at the boundaries: where negotiation and enquiry can take place freely, and where definition or defence is not necessary.

I recall one occasion where such 'space' was palpable in the college – in the court of Old Court itself – and the community was functioning at its best. The circumstances were tragic, following the death of a student from an accident while crossing the road. The funeral took place in the college: hundreds were gathered, and countless students participated. In the half-light of the late afternoon – after the crowds of guests had left and the formalities were over – were dozens of college members, from undergraduates to Fellows and including kitchen staff, lingering outside in the rain. Many did not know each other well but they trusted one another. Amidst the floral tributes there were tears, hugs and a profound sharing of grief. As the rain grew heavier they migrated back into the shelter of the Antechapel, where people sat in their exhaustion to talk over the day, to digest the week, to reflect in conversation together how life now looked and how it could be lived. Several commented to me later how, in those profound circumstances of a mixed community working together, crying together, talking together, even singing together – expressed in formal and informal ways – they were discovering a way forward and a shape of living. It was an emerging shape that acknowledged beauty and despair, life and death, Creator and creation – in the raw-but-real manner of Job and Ecclesiastes.

Intellectual Curiosity

Wisdom reflection is an *intellectual enterprise*. Those who pursue it suggest a deep, trusting curiosity about how things work, and a patience for observation. They hold together observed experience, ethical claims and persuasive speech. It is no wonder that some scholars believe that the wisdom teachers were a recognizable social force marked by elitist features.

This intellectual method does not commonly correspond to that of current academic enterprise in the sciences or the arts. Despite the commitment to observation and an assumption (at least in Proverbs) that reality assumes some constant and reliable patterns, it does not follow the bounds of any single discipline or field. Its gains cannot be commodified or examined – except over a lifetime. It sponsors learning for its own sake, not for any measurable goals or achievement.

Today's students are hungry for this element. Ever since Adam Smith (and since Margaret Thatcher more especially), education has been in danger of being reduced to a commodity, a product which professors sell to students. Thus any learning which cannot be counted does not count. Yet the soul of education is to be found in a lifelong cultivation of wisdom. This involves an inner journey as well as the outward one, which is thus partially invisible and cannot be quantified.

Such idealism concerning education still carries elitist overtones – with which Oxford and Cambridge are commonly associated. Yet even in these protected environments 'ideals and values' concerning education are replaced increasingly by targets and tables. The resulting commodification contributes to the undermining of collegiate life – with associated losses to the opportunities for interdisciplinary engagement, personal tuition and flourishing community.

The institutional structures, therefore, can no longer afford to encourage intellectual curiosity for its own sake. Those who work within those structures are thus less likely to offer their attention beyond the strict bounds of the intellectual commodity that is expected of them. It is not valued or rewarded. They thus invest less – and, when the clock strikes the hour, they withdraw and go home.

But the role of Dean is very different. The job description is less specific and thus the work is less easily defined and less readily completed. The post often carries with it an expectation of residence within the college – and thus of greater personal investment in the place and the people. The nature of the work

– both 'human' and 'divine' – demands the engagement of 'all your heart, mind and strength'.

This is a privilege and a demand. The need, however, is acute: especially in an environment where there are ever fewer colleagues who share the same vision for the integration of learning and for the community context in which this best takes place. Whereas – a few generations back – academics opened their homes for discussion evenings and organized 'reading parties' during vacations, such behaviour is now more often treated with suspicion. Perhaps such practices carry elitist overtones because they are costly – costly in the investment of intellectual curiosity as much as the investment of finance. But the wisdom teachers are not abstract idealists; they are pragmatists. This is their model for 'the best way to live' because any alternative is, ultimately, more costly.

Theology

Wisdom teaching is *theological literature*, even though it does not look like it. That is, it speaks of God; it helps us understand who He is and how He works in the world. What is unusual about this, however, is the way that it does this: not through religion, ritual or regulation, but through riddles, through experience and through speech. To those on the outside, therefore, the pursuit of 'wisdom' is perceived as far removed from the pursuit of 'religion' – yet this is not so according to the biblical, canonical tradition. Rather, the wisdom teachers encourage us to observe and reflect upon a world order that is willed, governed, and sustained by God – even when God seems absent or invisible.

This has appeal and relevance for those on the outside of faith. Such an approach functions, therefore, as an introduction to faith – helping people to relate to God by relating initially to the world which he created and engaging with matters pertaining to how to live well within it. It appeals to two characteristic features of the postmodern condition: the interest in nature and 'creation', in its widest sense, and the longing to establish a shape for living, a personal ethic, a basis for choice.

I do not mean to argue that wisdom theology is, in fact, a covert 'tool' for proselytism. It is no mere tool; and it is not covert. I am, however, suggesting it offers a way in to the Judaeo-Christian tradition that resists contemporary stereotyping and thus allows for creative engagement. This is as true of its method as its substance. By its nature it encourages questioning and refuses to prohibit the unacceptable; there is room for mystery and unanswered questions and loose ends – so long as there is reflection and conversation and trust. The detail concerning trust is fundamental to its effectiveness since, in my experience, it is no longer the case (if indeed it ever was) that a person may simply be *reasoned* to a place of faith. As Graham Cray has written concerning contemporary youth discipleship, 'it is likely that many young people of no Christian background will start to belong to the community before they are sure they can trust the message about its Saviour and Lord'. [21]

At the same time, wisdom is uncompromising. First, the consistent message throughout is that 'the fear of the LORD is the beginning of wisdom'. Apart from this foundation there is no wisdom. If we want to know how to understand and to live successfully in the world then we must begin with YHWH and be in right relationship with him. To be wise we must root our life and thought in the Creator. If the major postmodern issue is that of identity,[22] then here is the beginning of the answer: that we are God's creatures – not creators who are free to make anything we like of our lives.

Yet this is only the *beginning* – the start of a journey of exploration and discovery that is creation-wide and life-long.

Faith is not a closed package delivered once and for all. Education (in its most liberal sense) and the exploration of all of life follow on from this foundation and beginning. For wisdom is not just a characteristic of YHWH. It is something that we are to search out and seek to possess – the pearl of great price – while also finding ourselves possessed by it, realizing that we are God's pearl.[23] Then wisdom will be manifest in our lives.

Second, the wisdom literature assumes that obedience follows from faith. Proverbs proclaims, 'This is the way. Walk in it', and Job does so: he carries on walking in it, even when everything has failed. This is a radical path of discipleship: where questions, doubts and despair do not prevent faith but become the substance through which it is exercised.

Christ walks in this way also, to its ultimate extreme. The wisdom theme is carried into the New Testament and developed in Paul's First letter to the Corinthians. 'Where is the one who is wise? Where is the scribe? Where is the debater of this age? Has not God made foolish the wisdom of the world?' (1 Corinthians 1:20). Paul declares that God has turned the world upside down through Christ's death: 'who became for us wisdom from God, and righteousness and sanctification and redemption, in order that, as it is written, "Let the one who boasts, boast in the Lord"' (1 Corinthians 1:30-1). As a result, Christ on the cross is now the lens through which all human experience must be projected and thereby seen afresh. If Christ is the *wisdom* from God, we are not surprised to find his call to discipleship subverting all human 'wisdom', power and wealth; in Christ we find 'God's foolishness is wiser than human wisdom' (1 Corinthians 1:25). Here is the final riddle of God, expressed in the language of metaphor and irony, typical of wisdom.

In the wisdom literature of the Old Testament we find an applied apologetic. The wisdom tradition witnesses to a world as it was intended by the Creator – marked by *shalom*[24] – and as

34

it has been redeemed in Jesus Christ, the wisdom of God. It also relates readily to a world of experience that is far removed from this: as seen, paradigmatically, in the experience of Job. This literature offers a resource for ministry: a model whereby the realities of disappointment and pain can be embraced together with the aspirations of wisdom and *shalom*. In the particular situation of college life that I have experienced at Clare College, I have found a particular relevance to these ancient texts for a postmodern context. Here is no conventional religion, no clichéd Christianity but an idiosyncratic approach that fosters conversation and community. Through such means outsiders have come to take seriously the claims of the Judaeo-Christian faith.

Notes

1 The term 'wisdom' can be used to indicate certain books which deal particularly with wisdom (evidenced by the frequency of the Hebrew term for wisdom, *hokma*), or it can refer to a movement in the ancient world associated with teachers or sages. In both cases, it denotes a particular understanding of reality that contrasts with other biblical books.

2 Two books from the Apocrypha, Sirach and the Wisdom of Solomon, also follow the literary forms of wisdom, but this discussion is limited to those within the narrower definition of the canon. Nor does this chapter focus on other Old Testament books in which there may be some material with links to the wisdom tradition – some Psalms, for example.

3 Birch *et al.* (1999), p. 377. I am indebted to this source for describing the characteristics of wisdom literature that provided the inspiration for this chapter.

4 This shift is represented by literary and canonical critics who tend to focus on the final form of a book more than its likely redaction history. For a description of these developments with regard to Proverbs, see Whybray (1995), Chapter 2.

5 Consider, for example, the comparison (e.g. Proverbs 25:11–14, 18–20) and the list (e.g. Proverbs 30:15b–16, 18–19, 21–3).

6 Hauerwas (2001).

7 Proverbs 1:7; 9:10; 16:6; 31:30; Job 28:28; Ecclesiastes 5:7; 12:13.

8   See Exodus 3 and 6; Exodus 19.
9   This language is informed by John Milbank. See Milbank (1993).
10 Such processes of socialization are well described by Berger and Luckmann (1976).
11 Ford (1997).
12 Ibid., p. xiv.
13 'Accreditation of Prior Experience'.
14 Israel's particular name for God, YHWH, is used frequently, but – save a few exceptions such as 'the Holy One' in Proverbs 9:10 – without the usual associations.
15 Such approaches are termed 'Virtue Ethics' or 'Narrative Ethics' within the academic field of ethics. See, for example, the work of Stanley Hauerwas.
16 This terminology is borrowed from Craig Bartholomew; see Bartholomew (2001), p. 11.
17 See Zeldin (1998).
18 The notion of 'public space' has been well developed in the work of the architect, Richard Rogers. See his (1995) Reith lectures, Rogers (1996).
19 I have frequently used the four 'wonderings' which are key questions in the methodology of 'Godly Play': I wonder what part of … did you like the best? I wonder what part of … is the most important? I wonder what part of … is really about you? I wonder what part of … could you have managed without and still had all the … that you needed? See Stewart and Berryman, (1989), esp. pp. 30-1.
20 On the role of 'space' in the educational process, see Palmer (1993).
21 Cray (1978), p. 23.
22 Ibid., p. 22.
23 Cf. Matthew 13:45, 'Again, the kingdom of heaven is like a merchant in search of fine pearls; on finding one pearl of great value, he went and sold all that he had and bought it.' For an exposition, see Williams (1979), pp. 48–53.
24 The Hebrew *shalom* translates as whole, safe, prosperous and just – as well as peaceful.

References

Bartholomew, C. (2001) *Reading Proverbs with Integrity*. Cambridge: Grove Books.
Berger, P. L. and Luckmann, T. (1976) *The Social Construction of*

Reality: A Treatise in the Sociology of Knowledge. Garden City, NY: Doubleday.

Birch, B. C., Brueggemann, W., Fretheim, T. E. and Petersen, D. L. (1999) *A Theological Introduction to the Old Testament*. Nashville, TN: Abingdon.

Cray, G. (1978) *Postmodern Culture and Youth Discipleship: Commitment or Looking Cool?* Cambridge: Grove Books.

Ford, D. F. (1997) *The Shape of Living*. London: HarperCollins.

Hauerwas, S. (2001) *With the Grain of the Universe: The Church's Witness and Natural Theology: Being the Gifford Lectures Delivered at the University of St Andrews in 2001*. Grand Rapids, MI: Brazos Press.

Milbank, J. (1993) *Theology and Social Theory: Beyond Secular Reason*. Oxford: Blackwell.

Palmer, P. J. (1993) *To Know as We Are Known: Education as a Spiritual Journey*. San Francisco: Harper.

Rogers, R. (1996) *Cities for a Small Planet*. London: Faber & Faber.

Stewart, S. M. and Berryman, J. W. (1989) *Young Children and Worship*. Louisville, KY: Westminster John Knox.

Whybray, R. N. (1995) *The Book of Proverbs: A Survey of Modern Study*. Leiden: Brill.

Williams, H. A. (1979) *The True Wilderness*. Glasgow: Collins.

Zeldin, T. (1998) *Conversation*. London: Harvill Press.

2

The Anglican Church as a Polity of Presence[1]

Ben Quash

The Human Calling to Be Present

I have used the word 'presence' in the title of this chapter, but I want that word to have certain specific content in addition to its normal associations. I want it to include the idea of acknowledgement or recognition. I am interested in the way that we, as human beings, are present to ourselves and to one other (which is another way of saying how we acknowledge ourselves and one another in a way that is authentic, loving and liberating). I am also interested in the way that God is present to us and we are present to him.

We fail, of course, all the time to give due recognition to others – to allow them to be really present to us as themselves. But we also fail to make ourselves recognizable to them; to show the truth of ourselves in a way that makes us really knowable and genuinely present to them. I think of this latter withholding – the withholding of ourselves, the refusal to give others any opportunity to recognize (or acknowledge) *us* – as a form of one-way looking. One-way looking is the attempt to avoid reciprocity: to look without being looked at; to have knowledge, and even intimacy, without presence or self-offering. It is, in that sense, a form of spying.

What I will argue is that the Christian life must stand against all forms of one-way looking; all such forms of hiddenness and denial. Our calling is not to withhold our presence from those around us. Our calling, as imitators of Jesus Christ, is to bestow ourselves; to seek ever-new ways of being more fully present to our brothers and sisters, and the people God gives us to share our lives with.

Dietrich Bonhoeffer, in his book *Life Together*, is an important conversation partner here, because of the magnificent reflections he offers on candid living; speaking the truth in love; openly confessing one's status as a sinner, but then receiving the truth of oneself as a redeemed person as well. This clear-eyed mutual ministry of presence (of recognition and acknowledgement of the truth about ourselves and our condition as human beings) is the only way, Bonhoeffer argues, to true community – godly community. Only by being present to one another in the light that God's truth sheds on us do our forms of human community progress beyond being what Bonhoeffer calls mere 'hot-house flowers', liable to wither away in an instant. Really Christian life together, Bonhoeffer says (perhaps a little heartily), grows 'healthily in accord with God's good will in the rain and storm and sunshine of God's outdoors'.[2] Bonhoeffer's profoundest insight of all, here, is that our presence to one another in true community – in this honest mutual recognition – is utterly simultaneous with God's presence to us. God's presence to us enables us to be open to one another in community. God empowers us to risk making ourselves knowable and recognizable in the way we need to be; to come out of hiding. And, conversely, the genuine community of Christ's people enables the individual to know and recognize *God* – God's presence. It mediates God. Thus God is made present in the community of truth and love; in the body of his Church. God's action makes possible true human community; true human community makes possible God's presence.

There is something bold to be said in all this about Christian anthropology. The Christian view of the human being – of what the human being is *for*, and of what his or her vocation is – is partly that he or she is made to be a *recognizer*. The vocation of the human being is, amongst other things, to *recognize*. This seems, for example, to be a fundamental insight of Karl Rahner's theology. All creation is oriented towards a fulfilment in God – through all levels and stages of being, from the primeval slime onwards – but it is uniquely the human being who is bestowed with the gift of consciousness, of knowledge of self. In the human being, the created order can *think* at last; it can think about itself. It can be present to itself, in a distinctive and higher way than through the fact that its parts are just materially lumped together. It can be present to itself in the medium of consciousness. It can also think beyond itself, towards God – and so God too becomes present to the created order in a new and higher way, through the medium of the human being. (This is almost a priestly vocation – mediating God to the world and representing the world to God in the medium of consciousness.) God through the human being, who is the priest of creation, becomes present in knowledge as well as (implicitly) in the stuff of being. We get a vivid representation of this high vocation of man – the vocation to be a *recognizer* – in the Genesis account of the naming of the animals. This naming is the human being's role in the context of the whole creation – no other part of creation can do this. In Adam's work of naming, we have an image of the created order recognizing itself, acknowledging itself, in recognition of God and in cooperation with God.

The vocation of being acknowledgers or recognizers, therefore, draws us into close cooperation with the will of God – when we perform the role properly. When we cooperate with the will of God, we discover the work of acknowledgement (or recognition, or naming) to be a ministry of truth and love. True naming, true recognition, can only happen when we acknowledge the fullness of God's presence in others (other beings, other people). That is another way of saying that it can only happen when we approach the other in love. Any name we give and any recognition we bestow *without love* will be a false or misleading name, and a misrecognition. When we *do* acknowledge and recognize one another in love, meanwhile, we are actually sharing in the divine life – we are more adequately reflecting the image of God. For God is himself a recognizer.

This is perhaps the boldest claim of all but it cannot be avoided if we take seriously the message of the farewell discourses of John's Gospel. These are passages which, more than any others in the Bible, show the trinitarian life to us. And the movement that we see is described as being like a movement of recognition, acknowledgement, love, presence. The trinitarian life is one of total mutual recognition and recognizability, total mutual acknowledgement and openness to being acknowledged; or, to put it another way, total presence. The Son truly sees the Father, and the Father truly sees the Son. Not partially; not with certain obstructions in the way, but completely. The Spirit looks into the heart of both, and knows and has access to all the riches of love and truth which are there. The Son does what he sees the Father doing; the Father receives from and is glorified by the Son. The Spirit abides in and with both, as they abide in each other. The Father is in the Son, as the Son is in the Father. The Spirit can make them known in their fullness because he lives in them and out of the heart of them. Perfect presence.

The human vocation, in the image of God, is to know even as we are known; to be utterly transparent to God; to hold back nothing from his recognition; to hide from God no longer, but to be totally present to him. This is achieved when we are conformed to the total mutual recognizability of the Trinity; the total presence of God to himself. 'Those who love me,' says Jesus (in other words, those who recognize me, acknowledge me, are present to me), 'will be loved by my Father, and I will love them and reveal myself to them. ... We will come to them and make our home with them.' Then, later, in Chapter 15, Jesus says to his disciples: 'Abide in me as I abide in you. If you keep my commandments, you will abide in my love, just as I have kept my Father's commandments and abide in his love.' Then, in Chapter 17, we encounter that great appeal of Jesus Christ to his Father, even in the teeth of his betrayal and crucifixion: 'Father, glorify me in your *presence*' (verse 5; my emphasis). The implication of this is that Jesus' glory – the glory as of the only-begotten Son of the Father – derives from the fact that he is totally present to the divine life, and the divine life is totally present to him. He will be glorified in God's presence. His glory, which surpasses all glories, is a glory that comes from his perfect realization of the calling to be present to God, and in being present to God, to be present also to others.

I have been painting on a huge canvas in this last section. Now I want to link some of what I've been saying to Anglican life and recent events in the Anglican Church.

Embodying Presence in the Anglican Communion

The Primates of the Anglican Communion met in Portugal in 2000, with a difficult agenda and under a great deal of pressure. I was at the meeting with Professor David Ford from Cambridge, preparing material for three sessions in the early part of the meeting: a Bible study of the letter to the Ephesians which went deep into themes of holiness, hope, and the nature of the Church; and then two subsequent sessions that drew out these themes into a consideration of the Anglican interpretation of Scripture and the nature of Anglican polity. The meeting, I have to say, was fascinating and encouraging – far more encouraging than the reports of it in the press gave it credit for. Looming large in the background of the meeting was the question of the irregular consecration of two bishops in Singapore, to fly back into the Episcopal Church in the United States and minister to Anglicans alienated by the actions of certain bishops in that province – in particular, their blessing of same-sex unions and their ordination of practising homosexuals. Many people felt in the run-up to the meeting that these actions – on both sides – would prove to be Church-dividing issues: that they would split the Communion. What this threat forced the meeting to explore was what constituted the *unity* of the Church; what could enable it to remain in a state of mutual acknowledgement and mutual presence in the body of Christ, even in the face of impaired communion, and serious dispute over doctrine and practice. Thanks to Rowan Williams – who was there as the new Primate of the Church in Wales – the category of mutual recognizability came very much to the fore. The bare question (as he put it) was this: are we really prepared to say that Christians who are united in their affirmation of a single baptism in the threefold name of the Trinity, of the authority of Scripture in matters of doctrine, of the creeds of the undivided Church, and of episcopal ministry are not mutually *recognizable* to one another as Christians when they differ on matters of sexual ethics? If all these things are shared, are we saying of those with whom we disagree on other matters that we are unable to recognize them as fellow *Christians*? What does it take for someone no longer to be recognizable as a fellow member of the body?

The Primates' Meeting – at which, in face-to-face encounter and conversation, I found there was real mutual recognition, acknowledgement and humility (real mutual *presence*) – decided that it would take more than disagreement over sexual ethics to bring them to a point where they could not recognize one another in the body of Christ. Instead, there was among them a real passion to remain present to one another.

What they recognized and articulated early in that meeting is worth reiterating here, for it has to do with the deepest truth of the Church – as Ephesians powerfully presents it. David Ford, in one of his three talks to them, put it like this: in Jesus Christ, 'something has happened'; a new thing has been created. The wall of division between Jews and Gentiles – a divide which was 'religious, ethical, racial, cultural, political all together' – has been abolished. So the 'basic reality of this in all situations of division is that we are in one undivided space defined by Jesus Christ' – and this is the reality we must try to live by before God.

> This space 'in Christ' is worth meditating on deeply. What are its boundaries? In time, the holy ones are traced back to God's choice before the foundation of the world and forward to the fullness of time. What is outside 'the full-ness of him who fills all in all'? What is outside 'every family in heaven and on earth'? What is outside 'the breadth, length, height and depth of the love of Christ'? It almost takes away our category of outside. Admittedly not quite – there are still sin and evil. But really destroying this unity is made unthinkable.[3]

It is in this context that we seem compelled to acknowledge our presence to each other, rather than seeking to deny such recognition. The reality of the single space created in Christ to which Ephesians testifies is a reality that 'gives confidence that peace-making is always worth persevering in, whatever the difficul-ties'. The cross, of course, is:

> the measure of the difficulties, the pain, the shock and the horror that we may have to go through for unity. In

emphasising the cross, and Christ's flesh, body and blood, we are reminded that his peacemaking happens in sheer vulnerability, in weakness: it happens on the cross and not in the disputes with the Pharisees.[4]

Yet the cross, and the name of Jesus Christ, constitute 'our basic identity as a community' – an identity more basic than any other – Jew or Gentile, slave or free, male or female. We all stand at its foot. And, finally, 'there is nothing beyond the reach of the cross or the relevance of the cross' – the great *oikonomia* of God's grace evoked in Ephesians has this truth at its heart. We cannot run away from it, or from those who stand under it with us. In running away from them, we are running away from ourselves.

The Primates chose to affirm all this in continuing to affirm their mutual recognizability. They rejected a schismatic mind-set which has a nasty tendency to become an ecclesial habit. They agreed to allow the provinces most implicated in present difficulties to use their greater nearness to and understanding of those problems to try to address them – *trusting* them to exercise the ministry of unity with which they are charged in the wider context of God's Church. And all this was done with honest speaking and generosity and seriousness. This was *not* a cop-out. This was *not* sitting on the fence. It was a Church that knows more about its difficult vocation in the world than to think that there are short cuts to blessing; that you can ever carve out a pure part of the Church and discard the rest; that you can forgo the sacred, sustained conversation and mutual acknowledgement that is the life of Christ's Church in the world.

I want to follow these themes up in the remainder of what I say because I believe that the Anglican Communion is a part of the Church that very particularly and impressively fulfils the vocation of *presence*: it's close to the heart of Anglicanism, and needs to be cherished.

'Embodied, Contextual and Personal'

One of my fellow Deans in Cambridge, and a fellow contributor to this book, is Timothy Jenkins. As well as being a priest, he is a social anthropologist, and many of the things he says and writes arise from a training that is both anthropological and priestly. This often gives him very particular insights and a different language for expressing things.

Jenkins has a lot to teach us about the importance of good description – not description from a distance; not the imposition of alien categories or prior theories on what is before one; but description that begins 'by paying attention to the orderings made by the objects of our interest, rather than beginning from our own orderings'.[5] The sort of knowledge that emerges from this approach will be, to use his words, 'embodied, contextual and personal'.[6] Being able to develop descriptions of that kind is what makes a good social anthropologist. It's also, I think, part of the vocation of Christians, and perhaps especially of Christian ministers.

Let me quote some of what he has written on this subject:

While I was doing my curacy, I was greatly helped by my fieldwork experience, and this in two respects: on the one hand, in the techniques learnt of paying attention, and the other in the sense of not expecting to be needed. Anthropological experience and the business of Christian ministry correspond quite well in certain respects, or so it seems to me; for as an anthropologist, one's job is not to make all the difference, but to learn to see differences at work. So is a Christian minister required to pay attention: not to bring God into a situation (as – I am sorry to say – certain of us fresh from theological college had a tendency to believe), but to learn to discern his work and presence in a place.

And the other side of that is seeing that you yourself are not necessary to the situation: a clue to discernment is self-effacement. In fieldwork, that is obvious, for the problem is rather to learn to discern what effects are due to one's presence, and to discount them; it is not one's task gloriously to cause endless alteration. But the same is true, in a less obvious way, for the priest. This is partly to repeat the psychological point already touched upon: some young priests tend to flee from their superfluousness, their not being needed, by activism, through being useful. And it is partly upon theological grounds, for the grace of God is not found fundamentally in uses, or the meeting of needs. Christian worship, for example, is – if I may put it so without being misunderstood – thoroughly useless, in the technical sense that it meets no human ends. Practical necessity is therefore not a good clue to what the Christian life in a place is doing. But as an anthropologist, I was well-reconciled to having no useful task in a place, to being neither needed nor, necessarily, liked, and to spending my time instead watching, paying attention and, in particular, noticing when I was not getting things right; when I was not understanding.[7]

Jenkins observes, too, that his anthropological training enabled him to do some very specific things better, like conduct funerals.

It is worth noting here how linked this account of parish ministry is with the idea of presence. The parish priest is often in the very privileged position of being able to describe what the truth of everyday life is in a particular locality. In funerals, he has to describe the truth of a single life. His presence to the locality and to individuals and families authorizes this kind of description. The clergy describe well because they are really present to the situations they describe. In the words of Tim

Jenkins I used a little earlier, they have a knowledge which is 'embodied, contextual and personal'. This is a high and precious form of knowledge denied to outside observers, commentators and statisticians.

This leads me to two further points about the Anglican Church; first at the national level and then at the level of the Communion – points which pick up the reference I made earlier to the way that the Anglican Church is particularly good at fulfilling the vocation of presence. In many ways, it has tried to be a polity of presence – as present to the world as it can possibly be – by avoiding certain options. I am taking for granted here a belief that the Church is called in every age and place to maximize its presence to the world – for the sake of the world's salvation. It is charged, as Dan Hardy has put it, 'to place the intensity of the gospel in the closest affinity to those lives and societies to which it is addressed'.[8] Even when this requires 'critical distance from them, and prophetic engagement with them',[9] nevertheless *bringing the Gospel close* is what is in view. According to Hardy, the Church 'must be close to those to whom [it addresses itself], thinking their thoughts in order to find the intensity of the gospel in their forms of life, and expressing the Gospel in a manner that touches the deepest aspects of their lives'.[10]

First, then, some remarks on the Church of England's presence to the nation.

The Anglican Vocation to Presence

Presence to the Nation

Have you noticed the way that the Church is often almost completely invisible in the national newspapers? When it does appear, it appear as an *oddity*: either it will be the source of some eccentric or comic piece of news, particularly in the so-called silly season (the Bishop of Hereford being bitten by a pig, for example); or a scandal will be seized upon, usually sexual (with the implied subtext: 'Well, what do you expect from someone already so peculiar as to spend his time hanging round in churches?'); or the Church appears as a form of peculiar interest group, defending strange pieces of legislation on grounds that nobody else understands. If you arrived in England from another planet and wanted a description of the truth of the nation's life, and you read the national papers to find such a description, little would indicate to you that the Church played an important role in the nation.

If, on the other hand, you arrived from another planet and decided to begin by reading the *local* papers, you would get a totally different impression. 'Vicar tackles council on care for the elderly'; 'Church of England school stages pageant on the history of St Andrew's to raise money for village centre'; 'Churches together in St Neots to coordinate town's millennium celebrations', and so on. In the local press, the Church's role in community life – providing care, taking responsibility, focusing local activities, and all the rest of it – is described and acknowledged. In this context, there is nothing *odd* about the place of the Church. It is almost never portrayed as a form of peculiar interest group. Quite the contrary, it is an intrinsic part of the local scene, and one of the main points of reference for people in a particular place. In a curious sense, the local priest and the local paper have quite a lot in common – and sometimes recognize it. They are both identifiably proficient describers of their locality, and are both people who do their describing on *behalf* of the community. Almost the only time that the national media recognize this local proficiency is when there is some local disaster – a bomb or a rail crash or an abduction – and then, suddenly, the local priest is interviewed to express the feelings of the locality. It is as if a different paradigm has suddenly clicked into place, temporarily, before we revert yet again to stories about loony fundamentalists and naughty vicars. This was impressively evident in the midst of the horrific events in Soham in 2002, when Holly Wells and Jessica Chapman were murdered. The parish church became a place where several crucial things found articulation: the girls were described faithfully; the needs and wishes of their parents were sensitively registered and transmitted in a way that the feverishly excited news media failed to accomplish; and the grief and compassion of the community had a place to come to expression. All of this was done in the context of the Church's regular practice of setting human needs before God in prayer. The parish priest, Tim Alban Jones, emerged as a figure of good judgement, responsible speech and Christian assurance.

The explanation of why for the rest of the time the national press trivializes or takes only a prurient interest in the Church (discounting thereby any idea that it is an institution of importance to the nation) is perhaps partly that those people in the national press who take it upon themselves to describe the nation to itself are only partly present to it. This is because they mostly live in specific areas of London and drink in the same bars, and eat in the same restaurants, and they generally just talk to one other.[11] If you wanted a really *good* description of the nation's life, in my view, you'd be much better off asking the nation's clergy: the people who visit the nation's schools and hospitals and take its funerals and so on.

This 'contextual, embodied and personal' knowledge which arises from the parish priest's presence to a locality is then taken up and stored at other levels – in deanery chapters and at diocesan level. There, in the person of the bishop, it combines with insights that come from the things he is particularly present to at regional level. Presence to things at a different level of ordering enter the picture here: just as important in many ways, as what parish priests are present to at their local level. Bishops are present in a distinctive way to the life of the region, as well as to important parts of national life. And then, in turn, this accumulated wisdom of presence from across the country feeding its way through the Church's own networks of communication finds itself embodied in the archbishops, who can seek to make this wisdom present at a national level, through institutions and contacts that are at yet another level of ordering. The archbishops, and especially the Archbishop of Canterbury, are present to the nation's life in a distinctive way, in contact with many of the instruments of government and national life. In them, the Church is present to the nation at yet another level. The challenge to archbishops is to carry with them at this level the descriptive knowledge of other levels that comes to them through bishops, and parishes, and also, of course, chaplaincies. In all these ways, the national church has an extraordinary presence to that part of God's world which it seeks to serve. It has proximity to hearts, minds and institutions.

The Communion as a Polity of Presence

In a sense, I have less to say about Anglicanism at the level of the Communion, because I have set out the pattern for understanding it already when talking about the national church. The Communion, made up of its various provinces, is the next level up again – putting it in slightly crude terms. It is the level at which Anglicanism seeks to be present to the world in its international, or global, reality. And it has to try to do this without losing any of that local presence or proximity which relates it to the hearts and minds of people in extremely different social contexts.

The Anglican Communion is capable of embodying a quite extraordinary contextual knowledge of world events, because of the way its presence to localities across the world is gathered up and shared at Communion level. The plenary discussions on Islam and debt at the last Lambeth Conference, for example, and the discussion with Clare Short on debt at the Primates' Meeting, witnessed to the Anglican Communion's informed and authoritative power of *description*. When Islam was discussed, bishops from different parts of Africa, the Middle East, Pakistan and England (Bradford, to be precise) gave statesmanlike addresses on the situations in their regions, each of them sensitive to the local complexities as well as to the larger issues. You could see an Anglican wisdom being developed to meet one of the situations that, as David Ford pointed out to the Primates, 'has clear potential to devastate our world in the next millennium' – as we have already seen in the Balkans, and are seeing still in Indonesia, the Sudan, Nigeria, Pakistan and in numerous other places, and in the so-called 'War on Terror'. Something of the same quality was seen in the deliberations about international debt. The reason that Clare Short flew to Portugal to be with the Primates, and the reason that she and Gordon Brown and others spent a very significant amount of time with bishops during the Lambeth Conference, is because of the authoritative description they are together able to give of world realities, to which they are present on the ground in various places. Government policies around the world have quite definitely been influenced as a result of such encounters with the Church's descriptive power. And, incidentally, it is worth remarking again on how different an impression you will get of the world if you listen to the Primates of the Anglican Communion describe it, from what you will get if you read the national papers for a description of what is most urgent, outrageous or hopeful in the world. How many pages of the papers are given to news about the two-thirds world, in proportion to news about sex scandals, or the Oscars, or whatever? Not much. We should ask, occasionally, whether the world the newspapers make most present to us is the world to which God is most present.

This discussion of the Anglican Communion's significant way of maximizing its presence to the world is not meant to be a complacent one. I am not just interested in singing its praises. It is, of course, patchy, sometimes corrupt, and full of anomalies. In Dan Hardy's words, there is a definite need 'to generate greater "common ownership" of the Anglican Communion beyond that which can be brought about through the Archbishop of Canterbury'. It is lack of 'common ownership' which 'presses the Archbishop into a stronger role than previously', and in turn reduces the kind of common responsibility the member churches themselves feel obliged to exercise. '"Common ownership" will require each province to have a *modus vivendi* that intrinsically includes a moral obligation for the Communion as a whole.'[12] There also needs to be a common recognition of the place of its decisions and actions in relation to other Christian churches and denominations, and responsibility must be exercised here too. There is no question at all that there are major forces arrayed against Anglicanism's mode of sustaining communion. It needs ways of renewing and developing its shared understanding, feeling, imagination and practice, and of remaining in significant communication.

It is, however, impressive, and worthy of being cherished, because of its commitment to being the Church *in the world*, to *presence*. To put it in simple terms, it could have followed two paths, both of which it rejected. It could have been congregational, or sectarian, in form; or, in a closely related step, it could have stopped short at a provincial level, resulting in a set of merely national churches. This, frankly, would have made it a Church less present to the world than the Anglican Communion presently is. There is a level of world reality which is unavoidably global. More and more human activities, as Hardy points out, 'are pursued through global interconnections' – activities he calls '"world practices" – ecological, economic, communicational and cultural'. A Church that cannot be present to these realities is less present to the world than a Church that can. The structures of the Communion allow realities like Islam and debt to be embodied in true and authoritative descriptions, shared at an appropriate level; and I might say in passing that the world can be helped to address these realities with the help of such a Church. The form of the Anglican Communion is, I think, stronger than the form of a world federation of churches, though a federation can achieve many of the same things.

The other path which Anglicanism has so far rejected is that of strengthening central instruments of decision-making, Church government and teaching. This makes it messy, as everybody recognizes. On the other hand, once again, it makes it more present to the world it seeks to serve. It allows its various dioceses and provinces proximity to the ways of the peoples, regions and nations for whom they are responsible. It allows those provinces and dioceses to make certain decisions about their activity and pastoral care on the basis of their unique, local, embodied, contextual presence to those situations; thus (so the Communion trusts) 'placing the intensity of the Gospel in the closest affinity to those lives and societies to which it is addressed'. This is not an easy path to take – and strong instruments of unity are certainly needed, as everyone, I think, recognizes. It may very well be that the Pope will have an important role to play in safeguarding such unity in the future. But strong instruments of unity must also be sensitive and flexible, and embody trust. We do, after all, serve a God who trusts people to do his work for him and seeks to enlarge their capacity to do so. Some of the ways in which the Curia and the Congregation for the Doctrine of the Faith have operated even since the Second Vatican Council have not expressed an intense presence to the world. Centralized activity can be distant activity, not responsive to local descriptions of how things are. The ambiguity and lack of support with which many of the local Roman Catholic Church's initiatives in Latin America have been treated in recent decades are cases in point.

Conclusion

There are powerful forces in our society that tend towards breaking down reciprocity, and so diminishing our mutual presence. The problem of one-way looking – of the absence of presence – has to be situated in a broad context: the context of a society in which the lack of reciprocity seems endemic. To see the truth of this, as Oliver O'Donovan points out,[13] one need only look at the way our society is presided over by organs of *publicity* – especially advertising and the news media, and also the cult of celebrity – that abuse our basic need to *appear* before one another (to be acknowledged; to have recognition) by commodifying and packaging human beings and displaying them to us in a way that is utterly non-reciprocal. Publicity is a distinctively modern way in which we are supposed to become known to one another, but it is a 'roaming spotlight'[14] that selects its subjects with apparent arbitrariness and makes tokens or fictions of them. Those who look at them *spy* on them: it is one-way looking; intimacy without any self-bestowal. Its subjects die of it – often quite literally. The state of publicity is too lonely for them. Others cynically use it to hide the truth about themselves for their own short-term advantage.

How can we maintain a quality of true community in the midst of such pressures? There is more need than ever for high quality face-to-face communication. Otherwise we are vulnerable to all sorts of distortions and manipulations of the truth, or even just a sense of superficiality, a sense that we are never really fully in touch with other human beings.

Publicity represents just one set of the powerful forces in our society which tend towards breaking down reciprocity, and so diminishing our mutual presence – making us all spies on one another. The Church struggles against these forces to maintain mutual acknowledgement (despite its differences, and despite the highly politicized polarities enforced and perpetrated by the impatient and unsympathetic media). The Primates in Oporto enacted a properly Anglican form of polity – a polity of presence – inasmuch as their deliberations struggled to see behind the misrecognitions and misrepresentations of one another which were being peddled by newspapers and Internet sites and right-wing American pressure groups, and instead to listen to those genuinely present to the issues, exercising responsibility in their various localities, and to listen to them *while in their presence*. In other words, the Church struggled to fulfil its vocation of enacting real presence, and it is profoundly important – for the world's sake – that the Church continues to offer this example in an environment that is losing the ability to foster presence, and in which (unless an alternative is offered) no salvation will be offered to the world, only death. For presence to one another in truth and love is not just a vocation at the individual level. It is a vocation to the Church as a whole (and, indeed, to whole societies, for whose benefit the Church tries to structure and live out its forms of 'life together'). Anglicanism continues to have a great deal of wisdom to offer about how to realize such a vocation. If we cannot shape a Church in which people are genuinely present to each other, we have nothing to offer the world. If we can shape such a Church, we make the trinitarian life itself manifest in our midst.

Notes

1   An earlier version of this chapter was published in *Third Millennium* 5 (July 2002). I am grateful to Neil Chambers for his comments on an earlier draft of this chapter.
2   Bonhoeffer (1954), p. 24.
3   Professor David F. Ford, Address to Primates of the Anglican Communion (March 2000) Oporto, Portugal.
4   Ibid.
5   Jenkins (1999), p. 5.
6   Ibid., p. 18.
7   Paper given to the Cambridge Theological Society, Divinity Faculty, Cambridge (February 2000).
8   Hardy (2001), p. 148.
9   Ibid.
10 Hardy (2001), pp. 148–9.
11 The extensive and often intelligent coverage given at the time of his appointment as Archbishop of Canterbury to Rowan Williams' views and potential influence may be a sign that the trend can be bucked – although even here one cannot avoid the suspicion that for some commentators it will be because he is a charismatic individual rather than because the institutional forms of life and belief he represents are felt to deserve serious consideration that he will be given media space. (The late Cardinal Hume was treated similarly.) This will not be his fault, and it will almost certainly be a problem he seeks to address.
12 Hardy (2001), p. 149.
13 O'Donovan (2000).
14 Ibid., p. 22.

References

Bonhoeffer, D. (1954) *Life Together*. London: SCM Press.
Hardy, D. W. (2001) *Finding the Church: The Dynamic Truth of Anglicanism*. London: SCM Press.
Jenkins, T. (1999) *Religion in English Everyday Life*. New York and Oxford: Berghahn Press.
O'Donovan, O. (2000) 'The concept of publicity', *Studies in Christian Ethics*, 13, 1: 18–32.

Part II

Inquiry

3

'I Am the Truth': Text, Hermeneutics and the Person of Christ

Maggi Dawn

Introduction

In this chapter, I shall address the fact that current ideas concerning the interpretation of text threaten traditional notions about the Bible as the word of God. As a religion 'of the Book', it is important for the Christian faith to maintain confidence in its holy Scriptures. But new ideas about text seem to threaten the notion of a holy or inspired text. This is not a new problem, however, and accounts of how Christian thinkers have handled similar shifts in the intellectual landscape before us may give us courage as we seek to negotiate our relationship to text – and the Bible in particular – in a way that is both intellectually credible and supportive of our faith. I shall argue that rather than taking a defensive position, protecting the Christian tradition against the ingress of new and apparently dangerous ideas, we are called to engage with new ideas to the extent that Christian theology might offer new ways forward in hermeneutics.

The Church, the Academy and the Written Word

For many centuries, a recurring battle has been fought to prevent the Church and the university dividing over the development of Christian thought. Ever since the rise of the universities in the thirteenth century, the relationship between intellectual development and the practice of faith has presented Christian thinkers with a struggle – a struggle that from time to time has erupted into a crisis. From the point of view of the university, theology has not always been readily accepted as a truly academic endeavour. St Thomas Aquinas was among the first to wrestle with this problem, arguing with great passion that, not discounting the element of mystery and revelation in theology, it did nevertheless qualify by any accepted standard as an academic subject, and should therefore be recognized by universities. Aquinas was concerned that theology would have its scope narrowed progressively, being deemed important only for those areas of knowledge that had not yet been uncovered – in other words, he was taking preventative action against a 'God of the gaps' theology.

At the turn of the twenty-first century, Aquinas's fears seem to have been realized to a certain extent. The prevailing trends of thought in our culture no longer regard theology as central or even relevant at all – indeed, much work in philosophy, literature and science is based on the assumption that theology as part of the academic enterprise is only of historical value; theology, if it is acknowledged at all, is often considered a matter of private faith, not public relevance.

While theology faculties wrestle with these problems, the Church, week by week, is dealing with another set of problems, also produced by cultural shift: leading communities and running centres of worship in a world where adherence to the Christian faith is declining. Reports vary in their pessimism, but we are threatened, as a church, with complete decline in our present institutional structure in perhaps as little as 50 years. It is tempting for a church in decline to become defensive, setting both belief and practice in stone. But many times before now the Church has been over-cautious about embracing intellectual developments, for fear that its basic beliefs are being threatened. Think for instance of the controversy surrounding the work of such thinkers as Galileo or Darwin. Theology is one of the places where divergent interests have to be reconciled; moral and intellectual concerns have to be balanced together, and new hypotheses assessed in the light of their consequences for accepted traditions.

Nowhere has this struggle been more keenly felt than in the area of hermeneutics: the way we interpret text, and particularly the texts that make up the Bible. Christianity is one of three major world religions that is known as a religion 'of the Book'. Our relationship to the written word, and the way in which we interpret text, are critical to our understanding of our faith. But the relationship between the Christian faith and the written word is by no means a simple one. Whenever there are fundamental shifts in the way we think about the human mind, and about the individual in relationship to society, the knock-on effect is a change in the way we think about text. Western thought has shifted dramatically in recent decades in all these areas, and traditional presuppositions about reading, writing and interpretation have undergone deep and significant changes. It is no longer assumed that agreement can be reached on the meaning of text; interpretation is far more individualistic and varied than before, the meaning of text is less tied to its authors' intent, or to the group that traditionally owns the text, and the ordinary reader is left with a sense of bewilderment concerning the interpretation of text.

Religious movements always have a degree of choice in how they respond to such shifts. It is quite possible for a religious group to avoid any serious engagement with change, and maintain its own point of view. But clearly, to the extent a group chooses to do this, they isolate themselves from the world in which they live, and the consequences of this are not merely intellectual but spiritual and practical, eventually affecting everyday choices – what clothes to wear, what technologies to adopt, and so on – reducing the extent to which they can easily interact with the world around them. Fundamentalist sects and conservative Christian groups notably isolate themselves by the way they approach text through retaining a literalistic approach to the Bible. Such groups often believe themselves simply to be taking the text at face value. This approach, while believing itself to be one that brings no 'baggage' to the text, in fact only shields itself from the fact that all hermeneutic strategies are founded upon cultural assumptions: just because these assumptions are unexamined does not mean they are not there.

The choice for a degree of isolationism is not necessarily motivated by intellectual naivety, or religious stubbornness. New ideas about our relationship to the written word do create genuine difficulties for Church doctrine and practice, and they cannot be resolved quickly or simply. There are, in addition, huge pastoral implications to the act of uprooting people from the comfortable and unchallenged notion that it is possible to reach agreement on the clear meaning of the biblical texts. Other factors complicate the picture: churchgoers deal with rapid and unsettling change at every level of their lives, and often they depend upon their faith, or their God, to be the one place where they can depend upon certainty and security.[1] For all these reasons, the Church has sometimes been too cautious in engaging with current intellectual ideas.

Academic theology, however, does not enjoy the luxury of such a choice. If it is to retain its academic integrity, it has to remain in touch with advances in other disciplines. In the case of the study of text, it is bound therefore to take note of new developments in philosophy, language and literature. It engages with other disciplines, though, under a certain sense of 'siege' – for a further significant change in the context of Christian theology is that both in the university and the world at large, theology is no longer assumed to be exclusively or even predominantly a Christian endeavour. Therefore Christian theology is somewhat self-conscious also in its dialogue with others. Dialogue can, and should, be courageous and challenging for all parties. But anxieties can occur, particularly for a theological tradition that has long been associated with imperialism; Christian theology therefore needs to find a voice in which it can be, concurrently, both confidently assertive in its own tradition, while genuinely engaging in open-ended dialogue. If it is too magisterial, it loses its power. On the other hand, if it is too polite, it loses its confidence.

The Church, the Academy and the Anglican Tradition

In the midst of intense pressures on both the Church and the Academy, then, it is essential for the survival of each that we maintain the advance of Christian theology as a joint endeavour. Academic theology that loses its connection to a confessional faith becomes self-consciously exclusive; Church theology, if it loses the rigorous approach to difficult questions championed by the Academy, will find its theology gradually reduced and simplified until it can no longer approach the searching questions of life in the world it inhabits.

The Deans and Chaplains of Cambridge University are in an interesting position with regard to this troubled relationship. Not all the chaplains come from the Christian tradition, but all are people who practise the faith we profess in the context of an academic community, so we are acutely aware of the need to shape the practice of faith in such a way that it retains both its spiritual and intellectual integrity. But by an accident of history, most of us are not only Christians, but also Anglican priests. And the Anglican Church has within its tradition a good model whereby academic theology and confessional faith hold together.

Anglicanism is built on a three-cornered foundation – an equal appeal to Scripture, to tradition and to reason. This has always been the safeguard of Anglicanism. The dependence upon Scripture keeps our faith rooted in the faith of ancient Israel and in the story of Jesus Christ. The dependence upon tradition gives it continuity – a steady and measured development, in step with, but not eclipsed by, that of the culture it is part of. And its dependence upon reason – its commitment to make the faith make sense in the light of human thought – prevents it from becoming a religious ghetto: the commitment to reason is a commitment to interact with the thoughts and ideas and cultural development of world we inhabit.

This three-cornered approach, of course, is not about holding together three separate concerns: they are not separate, they interact and affect each other completely. The commitment to reason and to tradition means that our tradition must be subjected to a historical analysis. The commitment to tradition and to Scripture means that new ways of reading – new hermeneutical theories – are embraced, but always with an eye to the continuity of the faith we profess. And the commitment to both Scripture and reason means that we have to account for our hermeneutical method: we cannot simply say 'the Bible says'; we need to account for our interpretation, and its application to the life of the Church in its present setting.

This, then, offers us a model for maintaining tradition while at the same time interacting with the cultural and intellectual climate of our generation. But in doing this, it is essential that we do not simply become defensive in our approach, seeking to apologize for Christian theology, or to protect it against threatening developments. In a world that challenges the credibility of our faith it is all too easy to retreat into our own history, and become intellectually defensive. But history shows that whenever Christian theology has been under serious challenge, its survival did not come through the defensive preservation of tradition, but by the bold engagement of Christian thinkers with new ideas, such that Christian thinkers became key figures in the development of these new ideas. Not only did they articulate the Christian tradition in new and fresh ways, but they also contributed to the wider intellectual sphere. So it was that such eminent figures as Augustine, John Scotus Erigena, Aquinas and Schleiermacher affected not only theology but philosophy too, and that Hildegaard of Bingen, John Donne, Samuel Taylor Coleridge, T. S. Eliot and others are remembered as much for their contributions to literature and the arts as for the way they shaped Christian thought.

We have seen, then, that when radical changes in thought seem to threaten Christian theology, it is best placed to face such a threat if it perceives itself neither as the victim nor the survivor of intellectual change, but rather as a driving force in intellectual development. And we can take courage from Christian thinkers in past generations who succeeded not only in preserving the integrity of Christian theology through dramatic intellectual developments, but also in actively shaping the intellectual landscape. In nineteenth-century England, Samuel Taylor Coleridge was one such figure. His story is not only an interesting moment in the history of ideas, but also an inspiration to present-day Christian thinkers who grapple with the problem of hermeneutics. Andrew Bowie has suggested that postmodern philosophy would do well to revisit the Romantic thinkers, since they grappled with many ideas that were similar in nature to our present philosophical crises;[2] I would suggest that there are parallels for theology, and that Coleridge in particular offers us not only a historical inspiration, but some keys to the continuing development of Christian hermeneutics.

Coleridge: Romantic Inspiration for
Postmodern Hermeneutics

In late eighteenth-century Germany the 'Higher Criticism' began to emerge within theological studies. New advances were
made in the study of ancient texts, resulting in methods of
biblical analysis that included form criticism and source criticism. These methods of literary and textual analysis claimed to
identify within the existing texts of Scripture signs of earlier
texts that had been interpolated, edited, or added to. The idea
that human authors were involved in some way in writing the
Scriptures was not new. But the idea that texts had been rewritten, updated and added to by later editors was a bridge too
far for many Church theologians, who feared that these new
methods of analysis undermined the idea that the Bible was the
inspired word of God. The result was a dramatic fracture
between the Church and the Academy in Germany. This split
was observed by the young Coleridge who, in pursuit of nonconformist ideas and Unitarian theology, made his way to Germany to read and meet the Idealist and Romantic thinkers of the
post-Kantian generation who were to become a major influence
upon all his later thought.

In engaging with the ideas of the Higher Criticism, and the
philosophical ideas that underpinned it, Coleridge came to the
realization that these new methods of literary analysis did not
necessarily undermine the idea of divine inspiration. Indeed, if
the ideas were understood and developed in the right way, they
would enhance the capacity for the biblical texts to connect the
reader to God.

Coleridge developed his ideas about the interpretation of text
throughout the early nineteenth century, writing about the role
of text as a conveyor of ideas, the responsibility of the author in
conveying ideas, and the reader's contribution to the text in

interpreting what they read. Many of the ideas now familiar to us as reader-response theory are found here in prototype.[3] Finally, in the early 1820s, Coleridge brought these ideas to bear upon the reading of Scripture, and in *Confessions of an Inquiring Spirit* he addressed directly the problem of treating the Bible as a special, or unique text. *Confessions of an Inquiring Spirit* was completed by late 1824, and read in manuscript form by many of his friends and followers, some of whom became primary exponents of his ideas. It was held back from immediate publication and eventually edited and published in 1840, after Coleridge's death, by his nephew, Henry Coleridge. It had a varied reception, some regarding it as a dangerous book, but a century later, universities and seminaries all over the western world were taking for granted the validity of the methods of textual analysis that developed out of the Higher Criticism; today those methods still form the backbone of biblical studies, and Coleridge is credited by many scholars as having averted in England a crisis of similar proportions to that which occurred in Germany.

Coleridge's effectiveness in 'mediating German thought to the English public, and biblical piety to modern minds'[4] is partly responsible for the fact that the Higher Criticism gradually became absorbed into biblical studies, forming the backbone of critical methods taken for granted in present-day biblical studies. The Church and the Academy did not split, despite later controversies; indeed, Claude Welch goes so far as to say that the avoidance of a fracture between the Church and the Academy following the publication of the controversial *Essays and Reviews* was largely due to the fact that Coleridge had already prepared the ground.[5]

The story of *Confessions* shows us, then, that when intellectual developments are engaged with fearlessly, thoughtfully and creatively, Christian theology can take an active role in shaping the intellectual ideas that impinge upon the disciplines with which it has much in common. But *Confessions* also offers some useful models of hermeneutical approach that still have application now.

Confessions of an Inquiring Spirit

In *Confessions* Coleridge sets out to demonstrate not only that new hermeneutical theories do not need to be feared, but that they must be embraced, for they are in part a response to changing theories of how the human mind works. It was the shift in thought concerning the human person as a subject, and the way in which the 'I' relates to other individuals and to God, that gave rise to the necessity for new theories about text: the one is predicated upon the other. It was against the background of a re-thinking of the interaction between human and divine minds that Coleridge arrived at a dynamic view of text itself. He challenged the idea that the written word was merely a container – a neutral means of conveying ideas from one mind to another. For Coleridge, the text had, in some sense, a life of its own – the text became part of the meaning of what was conveyed. He describes the language of the written word as 'not only the vehicle of thought, but the wheels'.[6] In other words, the content of a text cannot ultimately be separated from the text itself: how the text is presented has everything to do with the meaning it conveys, and this invests a dynamic quality to it. Coleridge expounded this by using the newly emerging language of biological science: for the first time, in Coleridge's lifetime, the concept of 'life' was not only used in the context of meaning 'not dead' but in the sense that life was organic or animate, as opposed to inorganic or inanimate. Applying this idea to the written word, Coleridge treats text as if it has some power for growth and creativity residing within it, rather than being a cold, sterile implement for the transfer of absolute ideas.

For Coleridge, then, the written word has the capacity to 'live' and speak, but it can be petrified into silence through a non-dynamic view of Scripture. An idea that was prevalent at the time was that God 'dictated' the Bible to its authors who, rather than crafting their texts with literary skill, were more like secretaries to God, simply hearing God's words and writing them down. Coleridge takes this idea apart, showing that if no creative role is given either to the author or the reader, then the text becomes dead or inorganic, like a statue that has all the appearance of a person, but no life. He likens this to:

> a colossal Memnon's head, a hollow passage for a voice, a voice that mocks the voices of many men and speaks in their names and yet is but one voice and the same! – and no man uttered it, and never in a human heart was it conceived![7]

The 'Memnon's head', a recurring image in Coleridge's writing, was one of the huge ancient statues of Thebes; it made a musical sound when touched by the sun's rays, giving the impression of an inanimate figure singing. Coleridge likened this to the effect upon Scripture of the idea that the words were literally the words of God. For such a theory disembodies the words of Scripture. Removing the sense that the words were spoken by someone and to someone, far from preserving the idea that they are the words of God, renders them lifeless and removes from them any personal quality, thus disenabling them as the means through which God might continue to 'speak'. To view the text as the divinely given 'words of God' freezes them in time, to one set of meanings which cannot transfer to another time and place.

Effectively, when this happens, the text 'loses its voice' – in other words, there is a reduction in the range of meaning that the text is able to render up. The opening up of a hermeneutic approach to Scripture that allows the words the freedom to be interpreted, and in a sense, 'written' by the reader, enlivens the text – enables it to be the means through which God speaks again and again.

This is the recognition of a dynamic relationship between the author, the text and the reader, and that the role of God's Spirit is not to dictate the text, but to interact with human minds in the writing, the translating and the reading of the biblical texts. It restores a 'voice' to the text, enabling it once again to embody God's voice.

'Like any other book ...'

Based on this idea of text, Coleridge appealed to his readers to cease treating Scripture with special interpretative rules, and to read the Bible 'as any other book'. This is not to suggest that Coleridge thought of the Bible merely as one book among many. But he believed that if we suspend the normal rules of language and interpretation when reading the Bible, we may believe ourselves to be treating it with a special respect, but in fact we are incapacitating its inherent ability to speak to us.

We need to approach Scripture with the same literary sensibilities as one would any text, asking what kind of text we are reading – is it history, poetry or law? Does the text itself claim to be recording the words of God, or is its internal claim that of a story being told, a human lament, or a record of events? Only if one reads the Scripture as literature, says Coleridge, does the text have the freedom to live, to speak, to inspire. Coleridge's critics took offence at this idea, accusing him of having a 'low' view of Scripture, and treating it 'only' like any other literature. But to treat the Bible as 'any other book', was not, for Coleridge, a diminishing of Scripture: rather, it raised Scripture to the level of immense reverence he had for 'any other book'. Words, for Coleridge, were as important in philosophy as they were in poetry: he was acutely aware that the language of great literature expresses more than we can know at any one time or place, so that the literature of one generation can speak insights unthought of to future generations, and this is as true of the Bible as it is of Shakespeare. In the light of this, his assertion that he would approach the Bible as he would any other book is not so scandalous, for as Prickett comments, '[Coleridge] approaches Shakespeare with greater reverence than Paley approaches Holy Writ.'[8] Rather than lessening the supremacy of the Scriptures in their revelatory capacity, then, Coleridge envisages that if the Bible is read with the same interpretative method as 'any other book', it will require no special apologetics to demonstrate that it is the word of God, for its uniqueness in witnessing to the revelation of God in Christ will be self-evident.

Dynamism and 'Voice' in Text

It can be seen from this that Coleridge's theory of inspiration is something much more complex than a means of validating the authority of the text. His theory describes an ongoing interaction between God's Spirit and the human mind, in which divine and human minds communicate through the medium of text. Authors, translators, editors and readers are all engaged in this interaction between the human mind and the spirit of God, so that inspiration is not a single act between God and the author, but an ongoing relationship between all of these at every reading of the text. In *Confessions*, Coleridge therefore offers his readers a theory of inspiration that is predicated on a pneumatology, and a hermeneutic theory which, I would suggest, can be seen as the precursor to much postmodern theory in that it recognizes the autonomy of the text itself, and is revolutionary in the amount of weight it gives to the interpretation of the reader in the creation of meaning.

This view of inspiration further indicates that Coleridge's theology is based on an underlying view of a God that is personal and alive. It is a difficult point to establish, on account of Coleridge's tendency towards highly abstract formulations and his sympathy with neoplatonic thought. But woven through his writing on Inspiration is a clear appeal to the idea that the text – and supremely the text of Scripture – is not a lifeless medium, but a means of embodying a voice, and that the relationship between minds set up by a dynamic view of text is one that is active and alive, not based on a dead letter. This is so much the case that the 'voice' he ascribed to text could even be lost, petrifying that text and severely reducing its capacity for the creation of meaning. For Coleridge, it is the acknowledgement of many voices within the construction of the text that gives it the ability to 'voice' the truth of God.

'Voice' in text is an idea that has gained a lot of attention in recent literary studies. When the texts of the Bible were written within cultures where the oral tradition was strong, and therefore even if reading were undertaken silently, 'hearing' the text was assumed.[9] Since medieval times, however, reading has gradually changed, to become predominantly a solitary, silent and visual activity, and there has been consequently a radical distinction between the written and the spoken word.

The recovery of the sense of voice in text has been explored by a number of scholars in recent years, from a number of different points of view. Mikhail Bakhtin, for instance, writing in the mid-twentieth century, asserted that the written word was immediately and directly derived from spoken language. This takes numerous different forms, which Bakhtin calls 'primary genres', and literary forms, or 'secondary genres', are 'composed of various transformed primary genres (the rejoinder in dialogue, everyday stories, letters, diaries, minutes, and so forth). As a rule, these secondary genres of complex cultural communication play out various forms of primary speech communication.' The speech genre occurs in 'forms that recur so commonly in written or conversational discourse that often, the speaker may not be fully aware of their lexical composition and grammatical structure'.[10] The identification of speech genres within a text reveals how the writer wishes to present herself, what effect she has upon her audience, how her audience affects her, and what social constraints exist in these rhetorical dynamics. Bakhtin's theory of primary and secondary genres does not replace recognized literary generic forms, but within those forms, facilitates further analysis of the active relationship between writer, text and reader. Thus, speech genres interact with recognized literary genres to nuance their anticipated effect. The 'voice' of a text, then, is not merely to do with the idea of accessibility, or of style. Rather, it is to do with the more fundamental issue that the underlying message of the text is conveyed by its form, which has the power to reinforce, nuance, or even subvert the apparent meaning of the text's content.

Voice in Text

This is highly significant for theology, for to understand text as 'voiced' implies that the form of a text is inherent to its meaning. If doctrinal truths are extrapolated from a text without paying attention to its form, then much of the meaning in the text is lost. The forms in which theology is voiced, then, cannot be separated from their content. How does this work? In the case of spoken language, we know instinctively that the voice instils meaning into the words we speak. Imagine a mother putting a small child to bed early in the evening. The bedtime routine finished, she smiles, kisses the child and says softly, 'Go to sleep, now.' The tone of voice, the look on her face, thread through the words other, hidden meanings: 'I love you, I'm pleased with you, all is well between us.' But three hours later, if the child is misbehaving and fractious, and the mother frustrated and weary, the same words might be spoken by the same mother to the same child: 'Go to sleep, now!' The words are identical. But the hidden meanings in the tone of voice this time suggest a different set of meanings: 'I am not pleased with you, all is NOT well between us, this house is not a peaceful place.' So, just as the tone of voice constitutes meaning in speech, so there is a sense in which written language has a 'voice'.

How does this awareness of voice affect the interpretation of text? An example is another *Confessions* – that of Augustine.[11] He sets out to explain to the reader how he arrived at the Christian view of God, and how he understands Christian doctrine. But he does so in a highly personalized form, writing in the first person, and addressing his words directly to God. The pages of his *Confessions* are peppered with references to Scripture, and especially to two parts of Scripture that are also voiced in the first person – the Psalms, and the letters of St Paul. By the end of the book, the reader has been taken through a personal account of Augustine's journey into Christian faith, stopping along the way to describe the principal areas of Christian theology and anthropology. The later parts of *Confessions* are more intensely and abstractly philosophical, but even here the form of address to God is maintained. To describe Augustine's theology point by point (as indeed we often ask undergraduates to do!) will supply a decent enough grasp of his theology. But the whole is nuanced by the form of *Confessions*, for the whole point of his account of Christianity is not to supply a philosophical system, but for the reader to engage, as he himself has, in a personal relationship with God. Read as a book of doctrine, the *Confessions* delivers a certain amount. But only with attention to the form of writing – the first person account, the interjections of thanksgiving and worship that are woven through the text, and the clear implication that the reader may follow Augustine into such a spiritual relationship – does the doctrine take shape and come to life.

It is for just these reasons that a dynamic view of text is essential to Christian theology, and supremely so to the interpretation of Scripture. For Christianity is not ultimately located in a philosophical system, or a particular religious practice, but a relationship with a living God. Only a dynamic view of text will deliver this possibility to us. A static view of text, conversely, restricts the possibility of text to allow for the personal revelation of God.

Voice, Dynamism, and the Person of Christ

The ground we have covered so far suggests to us that in order for Scripture to be able to connect its readers to the life of God, we must abandon the tendency towards a 'magic' or superstitious view of Scripture. Such a view leads to the veneration of the text itself, for, while intending to preserve the holiness of Scripture, it actually fossilizes the life of the text, silencing its voice. A miraculously given text – a text without an author – does not speak, and therefore cannot embody God's self-revelation.

There are, of course, difficulties in maintaining a dynamic view of text, for a fluidity in interpretation runs the risk of losing a communality of meaning. A dynamic view of the text with no means of focusing boundaries or critique runs the risk of the result ultimately being meaninglessness – any and every meaning being as indistinct as no meaning at all. But what saves biblical hermeneutics from disintegrating in this way is not so much a literary technique as a fundamental theological truth – that the 'Word of God' is not primarily expressed in the words of Scripture, but in the incarnation of Christ. For the Word of God is not primarily the written word, but the Living Word – Christ himself. Coleridge explored the idea of the *logos,* the Word of God, in a number of ways; and his theory of inspiration and hermeneutics as it appears in *Confessions* is predicated upon this idea. It is precisely in the double meaning of this concept that the key lies to allowing the text to have a voice: conveying some stable idea of truth, while maintaining a fluidity and dynamism of meaning. If the text recovers its voice, it is not because of a better literary theory, but because we see beyond the text to the person of Christ.

It is for this reason that Coleridge insists that the Bible itself is not an article of faith, but a witness to faith, and consequently we expect more of the text than a guarantee against heresy, a means of securing accuracy of meaning. For these things cannot exist apart from the person of Christ himself, and a hermeneutics that buttons everything up too neatly defies the purpose of Scripture in offering the self-revelation of God.

Both the person of Christ and the scriptural record are aptly called 'the Word of God', indicating that they are both means of revelation. But the Christian religion is predicated upon the basic idea that God is primarily concerned, not with imparting laws or morals or doctrines, but with communicating himself to his people. Thus the words of Christ reduce the ten commandments to two principles – that if you receive the self-revelation of God, the rules of life will follow from that without needing further explanation. As Augustine puts it, we may love God, and do what we like. But the converse is not the case – no amount of obeying religious rules will connect a person to the life of God. The initiative in knowing God always comes from God to us, not the other way around.

Conclusion: Christian Hermeneutics is about Development, not Defensiveness

If, then, as I suggested at the outset, academic and Church theology are to maintain a mutually supportive relationship, courage and mutual trust will be required from both sides. Christian theology lives in danger of merely defending its ground. The tendency of institutions in decline is to retreat, to dig in and preserve what we have left, preserving it forever in aspic. We cannot afford to do this: if we treat our intellectual tradition (as well as our liturgical and hierarchical traditions) as things to be defended and preserved, we will be dead, in every sense of the word, inside a century. But there is another way: if we treat our tradition not as something to be preserved and defended, but as something that is alive and growing, then the central truths and purposes of the tradition will remain rich and strong, and will inform its own development. And in this we should take courage from such thinkers as Coleridge who, rather than acting defensively in the face of new ideas, worked to shape the way those ideas were taken up, and in the end he was seen to succeed in providing a way forward with new ideas that were still faithful to the heart of the tradition.

The key to our relationship to text, then, lies in this conundrum: that the words on the page are alive to us only if we recognize that 'the Word of God' is not primarily a matter of the written word, but of Jesus Christ himself. When ideas concerning our relationship to text undergo dramatic changes, we have no realistic choice but to face the insecurity they bring concerning our ability to hold on to the absolute truth of God. But in order to keep our faith alive, we have to dare to focus our vision, not short-sightedly on the tradition as it has been handed to us, but on the living God whom text and tradition convey. Absolute truth is not found in formulations – even those as illustrious as the holy Scriptures – but in God himself. If we dare to step towards God on the shifting ground of intellectual inquiry, we will be enabled not merely to preserve the tradition as it was handed to us, but to continue it, to make it grow, and to keep it alive. For Christian hermeneutics to remain truly Christian, we must avoid treating text as a means of preserving a historical religion in terminal decline, and instead expect it to voice the living truth of Christ.

Notes

1   The relationship between fundamentalism or extreme conserva-
    tism and text is explored in Boone (1990).
2   Bowie (1977).
3   Coleridge (1818).
4   Drury (1989), p. 107.
5   Welch (1985), p. 16.
6   Coleridge (1825), p. xv.
7   Coleridge (1840), p. 1134.
8   Prickett (1976), p. 28.
9   The development of reading as a silent activity is usually traced
    back to the invention of the printing press, but Paul Saenger
    (1997) argues that the development of script-writing in medieval
    monasteries was every bit as significant to the separation of written
    from spoken language.
10 Bakhtin (1986), p. 98.
11 Augustine (1991).

References

Augustine (1991) *Confessions* (trans. and with an introduction and
    notes by Henry Chadwick). Oxford: Oxford University Press.
Bakhtin, M. M. (1986) *Speech Genres and Other Late Essays* (trans. V
    W. McGee). Austin, TX: University of Texas Press.
Boone, K. C. (1990) *The Bible Tells Them So: The Discourse of
    Protestant Fundamentalism*. London: SCM Press.
Bowie, A. (1977) *From Romanticism to Critical Theory*. New York:
    Routledge.
Coleridge, S. T. ([1818] 1969, 1991) *The Friend* (edited and with an

Introduction by Barbara E. Rooke). *Collected Works of Samuel Taylor Coleridge* (general ed. Kathleen Coburn). Princeton, NJ: Princeton University Press and London: Routledge, Vol. 4 i.

Coleridge, S. T. ([1825] 1867) *Aids to Reflection* (12th edn). London: Moxon,.

Coleridge, S. T. ([1840] 1995) 'Confessions of an Inquiring Spirit', in *Collected Works of Samuel Taylor Coleridge* (general ed. Kathleen Coburn). Princeton, NJ: Princeton University Press and London: Routledge, Vol. 11 ii.

Drury, J. M. (1989) *Critics of the Bible 1724-1873*. Cambridge: Cambridge University Press.

Prickett, S. (1976) *Romanticism and Religion*. Cambridge: Cambridge University Press.

Saenger, P. (1997) *Space Between Words: The Origins of Silent Reading*. Stanford, CA: Stanford University Press.

Welch, C. (1985) 'Samuel Taylor Coleridge', in N. Smart, J. Clayton, S. T. Katz and P. Sherry (eds), *Nineteenth Century Religious Thought in the West*. Vol. II. Cambridge: Cambridge University Press.

4

The Church of England and Evil: Active Optimism

Jack McDonald

The Problem of Evil and the Church

Not everyone in the twenty-first Christian century is sympathetic to the Church. This lack of sympathy is not expressed uniformly. There is a kind of soft atheist for whom English Christianity is a leisure activity about as diverting and morally serious as playing golf or going to the cinema. Because attachment to a church is no more serious than these activities, the soft atheist sees no reason why special privileges and respect should be accorded to the Church, which should more correctly be treated as a private and uninfluential club.

Not all opponents are as benignly tolerant of Christianity as this. There is a type of harder atheist who sees Christianity not just as gentle and harmless buffoonery, but as dangerous nonsense. The hard atheist might perhaps be tolerant of the Church's strange but irrelevant arguments over, for example, the correctness of saying *thou* or *you* in its tedious liturgies. After all, any private society is at liberty to indulge itself in such trivia. But – among other complaints – this materialist baulks at the Church's role as a source of cruelty and wickedness in the world and at its poor grasp of the nature of evil and of how evil may be combatted. In short, he argues that theism as represented by the Church is unethical.

The Church need offer no response to the soft atheist and his bewilderment at its bizarre private preoccupations like squabbling over inclusive language – it scarcely matters whether the vicar intones *men* or *humankind* in public worship to which few are drawn anyway. Atheists soft and hard must allow the Church its simple pleasures, even if these include internal grumbling intolerance. But where the Church must respond is to the charge that Christians have got it wrong about evil. Indeed, the very mention of evil injects welcome seriousness into the debate which the theist can have with the materialist. While it is fun to position religious arguments on inconsequential battlefields like churchmanship, inclusive language and gay vicars (or no gay vicars), in the end, a grave and fundamental issue like evil serves to focus both theist and materialist on a gritty and unyielding human phenomenon which, while it has on first reckoning naught for either side's comfort, still remains utterly central to human self-understanding.[1]

The Church's Addressing of the Practical Mystery of Evil Lends it Practical Credibility

Accepting an uncontroversial distinction by John Hick between the Mystery of Evil and the Problem of Evil,[2] we allow ourselves the remark that the Church has always looked coolly and closely at the Mystery of Evil – at the grinding business of living and coping with the reality of evil-suffered and evil-done. My colleague Ben Quash has written eloquently in this volume of the quiet, unglamorous and dogged work of the Anglican Church in being usefully present to local communities.[3] This quiet care shows itself most notably towards those in distress. And citing Anglican benevolence is not of course to diminish the impact of other Christian and non-Christian religious communities in this respect. The point is that religious faith is seen readily as a sturdy call to the alleviation of suffering.

As it happens and for historical reasons, the Church of

England finds itself particularly well placed to perform this humanitarian role in England. An obvious example is the ministry of conducting the funerals of a near-majority of the English dead and of undertaking the pastoral care of those bereaved in consequence.[4] Given the numbers involved, and the shaky church affiliation of the majority concerned, the Church of England is required to be open and unjudgemental in this daily confrontation with family suffering.

Coping with the Mystery of Evil has produced many imaginative interfaces between the Church and areas of significant national life. The basic ministry of parish clergy to anyone within a geographical area is complemented by specific ministries of care, for example, in hospital chaplaincy, which underline the practical commitment of the Church as an institution which is present self-consciously to serve those experiencing pain and suffering.

We have referred here only to the work of the clergy; and this is of course the mere tip of the iceberg. The entire Church finds a good slice of its practical reason for existing in striving to meet the needs of a tormented world. The happy rise in Britain since the Second World War of the welfare state, and of government and secular charities taking on the burden of this work of the alleviation of suffering, has not lessened the purposeful desire of Christians to be of useful and practical humane service.

The Christian addresses the Mystery of Evil not simply with charitable works. The liturgy and worship of the Church at funerals underline that this Mystery is indeed a *mystery*, incapable of being compassed by conventional human discourse. For most Christians, adhering to the public worship of the Church and to private prayer is the closest they come – and the closest anyone can come, from the theistic perspective – to addressing the Mystery of Evil.

The Problem of Evil Argument

The Church is prevented from any temptation to wallow in the Mystery of Evil by the bubbling up of the dark Problem of Evil to balance it. Evil is not just a set of grim experiences to be challenged, confronted, lived through and brought to worship. Evil is also unavoidably an intellectual problem. For example, it is insufficient in Christian terms to trumpet a Liberation Theology of God's special option for the poor and oppressed, and to work for social justice in society, without pressing this struggle to include the asking of hard questions about the reasons why the poor and oppressed are permitted by God to suffer the humiliations they do. Attachment to the public life and worship of the Church unaccompanied by this intellectual step results in a sort of Christian Shintoism – the primacy of religious ritual over reflective thinking. And such a response is an abandonment of a mature trust in an ethical theism as the underpinning of human life and experience.

Historically, Christians have not shirked this intellectual responsibility. Indeed, the vocabulary with which the discussion is conducted has been given to us by theologians, in the traditional categories of Natural Evil and Moral Evil, or variations on this theme like Herbert McCabe's Evil-suffered and Evil-done[5] or Leibniz's Metaphysical Evil, Physical Evil and Moral Evil.[6] Peter van Inwagen has categorized the problem as one of the Magnitude, Duration and Distribution of Evil.[7] It is largely Christian theology which has provided the West with the vocabulary and terms of reference for this argument.

The Church has also provided the intellectual stimulus to engage in it, partly because (as just mentioned) a satisfying Christian theology cannot stop at the Mystery of Evil, and partly to fill the conceptual vacuum of materialism's abrupt halt at the Mystery and its practical alleviation. The materialist, wedded to a metaphysic which isn't one (that is, to an account of the universe and mankind as the properties and powers of unintended physical matter) can have little of interest to say about the origins, rationale and purposes of the Mystery of Evil. The materialist's best move is to change the subject when some explanation of the Mystery of Evil is sought. In thus evading the issue, the materialist wilfully ignores the common experience of human beings throughout the ages, who have consistently demanded a proper and fundamental *explanation* for their sufferings. But a materialist response constructed on secular puritanical moralizing or saccharine sentimentality does not in fact answer our basic, enduring questions about evil. Christians too (emboldened perhaps by an impressive track-record of philanthropic care) are immune neither from puritanical moralizing nor from saccharine sentimentality; but the fact that the Mystery of Evil overspills into the Problem of Evil – which flatly demands an *explanation* to accompany the social work – is a helpful antidote to any such smug posturing.

We concede in advance that the Problem of Evil admits of no easy answer. Because of this, the resort to a purely fideistic or obscurantist response is tempting. But we bear in mind Leibniz's dictum that our theological explanations, although they may be *above* reason, should not be *against* reason.[8] On this notoriously difficult intellectual hinterland should therefore exist a delicate interplay between modernity's persuasive scientific method (in theology as elsewhere) and an openness to metaphysical explanations which will do personal justice to such difficult human experiences.

A Brief Statement of the Problem of Evil

Evil has always been a real problem, and not just a puzzle, for theists. It has never been an authentic theistic response to maintain that evil is merely illusory, or that it does not matter. Materialists have not been slow in claiming that this acceptance of the raw fact of evil may not easily be squared with other fundamental beliefs which theists commonly hold about the nature of reality. Specifically, it seems inconsistent to hold true all three of the following trilemma of propositions, first formulated by Sextus Empiricus in the second century:[9]

1. God is omnipotent.
2. God is wholly good.
3. Evil exists.

An immediate response is that close attention sees no formal contradiction in these three propositions; but if, with J. L. Mackie, we add two other premises further specifying the meaning of 'good', 'evil' and 'omnipotent', a necessary contradiction seems to arise:[10]

*   Good is opposed to evil such that it eliminates evil as far as possible.
*   There are no limits to what an omnipotent being can do.

With these two riders, it seems impossible to hold any two of (1), (2) and (3) without the third being false.

A Logical but Stark Theodicy: All Evil is Necessary

There is in this trilemma a certain philosophical over-simplicity, as we might expect from such a speedy knock-down argument against God's existence. In reflecting more closely, we see that the claim that God is all good is not true by definition. For example, it would be easy to hold that divine causal efficacy and power are more intrinsic to theism than divine moral perfection. Richard Swinburne is within his philosophical rights to wonder how on earth it was ever imagined that the God of theism should be expected to create the best of all possible worlds.[11] It is coherent theism to maintain that God's primary interest in the universe is physical, and that a moral dimension is an epiphenomenal effect of the incomparable physical structure which is God's chief gift. So the criticisms of Mackie and others are really just an argument against one simplistic theory of God's nature.

Nonetheless theists have, as it happens, claimed that it would be desirable to hold the two divine perfections of omnipotence and omnibenevolence together, and it seems straightforwardly possible to hold this, even given the existence of evil. There is a possible world in which there are trillions of great goods and one tiny evil, and in this possible world the trilemma is clearly not problematic for theism. It is, then, the magnitude, duration and distribution of evil which exercise the atheist. Even so, it is not obviously true that there are ultimately unredeemed evils – those which are in principle beyond any explanation compatible with God's existence. Indeed, it is obviously false that there are evils which are necessarily unredeemable. So all the theist seems to need to say is 'For all we know, all evil could be necessary.'

But the simple, knock-down theodicy 'For all we know, all evil and suffering are necessary', although it might be a logician's sufficient riposte to the materialist, has been seen to be a poor solution to the Problem of Evil. We are mindful of Fyodor Dostoyevsky's stinging practical rebuke through the mouth of Ivan Karamazov:

> Imagine that it is you yourself who are erecting the edifice of human destiny with the aim of making men happy in the end, of giving them peace and contentment at last, but that to do that it is absolutely necessary, and indeed quite

inevitable, to torture to death only one tiny creature, the little girl who beat her breast with her fist, and to found the edifice on her unavenged tears – would you consent to be the architect on those conditions? Tell me and do not lie.[12]

And Alyosha Karamazov's soft reply is 'No, I wouldn't.'

So even if theists believe that all evil is necessary and that no evil is unredeemed, there is a simultaneous nagging doubt – even among the faithful Alyoshas – that this proposition, even if true, is unethical and grotesque, given the immediacy and brutality of human suffering. We squirm when we think of Dostoyevsky's little girl beating her breast and on hearing some lofty theodicy in response to the effect that her suffering actually contributes to some ultimate good. We squirm still more when we contemplate Auschwitz or the Twin Towers catastrophe having to be justified in this way.

There are indeed some theists who take a deep breath and conduct their theodicy thus. A Richard Swinburne stares steadily at the innocent dying child as the victim of a necessary system and believes that God will ultimately redeem all evil and reveal his loving purposes, and that this consequence will justify the suffering,[13] whereas a D. Z. Phillips sees the dying child as bad enough, but the additional fact that God has intended the child to die in agony from eternity as exacerbating the evil.[14] To seek to justify the providence of God in the face of such a cavalier eternal plan is, for Dorothée Soelle, merely 'to worship the executioner'.[15]

So to hold that all evil is necessary is a logically coherent position, but it is scarcely in keeping with the fullness of normal ethical theism, in which a dimension applicable at the level of personal human experience has always been of central importance. It is a sort of theodicy for logicians, standing in need of an authentic theological supplement to flesh out its starkness in ways which soften and personalize it.

Fleshing out a Theodicy in an Unhistorical and Pessimistic Metaphysics: Genesis 3 and the Fall of Man

In attempting to produce a theodicy which is more theologically and personally satisfying than the logical version just outlined, we quickly encounter a real difficulty internal to Christianity of how to apply the teachings of the Holy Scriptures to the Problem of Evil.

Historically, the most popular Christian theodicy centres on an Augustinian interpretation of the biblical Fall in Genesis 3, according to which the first generation of humans rebelled against God and fell from a state of paradise to one of sinful alienation from God and consequent suffering.[16] The consequences of this original sin were then inherited by all human offspring, as also – via a method incomprehensible to any coherent human jurisprudence – was the guilt for it. All contemporary evil is held to result from this Fall, which is taken as an historical event.

When an opponent points out that this account does not actually *explain* the origin of evil, another mythological event, the Fall of the Angels referred to in other biblical texts is invoked to account for pre-human suffering.[17]

Such an interpretation of Genesis 3 is frequently (although not necessarily) allied to a Predestinarian Defence, which precisely wallows in the lack of free will which this inherited transference of original sin implies: our apparent free will is illusory. The nature of mankind is corrupted by the Fall, for which each generation of human beings remains responsible.

God in his 'goodness' has pre-elected a certain number to everlasting bliss and the rest to everlasting damnation.

If 'All evil is necessary' is a theodicy for logicians, then 'All people are fallen' is a theodicy for sadists and masochists. It bears no relation to our other knowledge of the world – in particular the insights of biological science are incompatible with the reception of Genesis 3 as an historical account of the origins of the experience of evil. It argues with all credible theories, both ancient and modern, of the assignation of guilt for wrongdoing. It therefore highlights the danger, once one travels beyond the cold frontiers of logic to the personal narratives of theology, of just telling stories (and thus exasperating our soft materialist), or for that matter of telling nasty and irrational stories (and thus offending our hard materialist).

The Fall therefore seems wholly unsatisfactory as the basis for a theodicy. First, we have no reason to suppose that it is true, and strong reason from our other knowledge to suppose that it is flatly untrue. Second, holding that it is true involves renouncing any meaningful claim that theism is ethical. Indeed, if the Fall as popularly received were true, this would confirm the hard materialist's claim that theism is profoundly immoral and that theism's God is a monster.

Fleshing out a Theodicy in an Ahistorical and Optimistic Metaphysics: Leibniz's Best Possible World

Theistic approaches to the Problem of Evil are not limited to those which are grounded in sacred texts and their narratives. Much of the vocabulary of the Problem is rooted in discussions which do not employ biblical terminology. A famous example of this unscriptural tendency is the concept of the Best Possible World used by the German mathematician, diplomat and phil-

91

osopher Gottfried Wilhelm Leibniz (1646–1716), which we now discuss for no better reasons than that the ingenious Leibniz is a particular favourite of mine, and that a gift which Anglicanism offers to the whole Church is an admiration for the theology of non-Anglicans.

For Leibniz, cradle Lutheran and cautious adult believer, religious narrative seemed much too loose and anthropomorphic a vehicle for expressing the whole truth of theology. Instead he sought more metaphysical rigour in a theodicy (the word was his invention) which, even if it employed biblical categories, was not dependent on them, and which would inspire general rational conviction.[18]

In the theological realm, Leibniz was essentially a metaphysician. For him, ethical worries about the moral implications of a theodicy were firmly subordinate to the metaphysical imperative of describing and explaining God's relation to the universe. This difference from the traditional Scripture-inspired method coalescing around differing interpretations of the Fall has the twin effects of producing a grander doctrine of God as well as a more optimistic one.

For Leibniz, God's power is limited only to the extent that he cannot perform logical or metaphysical impossibilities. God is the creator of the universe and not merely its architect. God creates from choice, not from necessity. As part of this thorough-going theism, Leibniz was also keen to repudiate a Manichaean dualism (also resurgent in eighteenth-century Lutheran piety, with its stress on the fallen state of mankind), according to which evil emanates from a devilish power. For Leibniz, the imperfections of the universe are produced neither by angelic nor human rebellion, but are metaphysically *necessary* to preserve its distinction from God. The universe is the Best Possible World, as perfect as it could be without dissolving back into God, and as perfect as it could be without being worse.

In Leibniz's resolution of the Problem of Evil, the entire universe is generated from Pure Being (that is, God) and whatever-is-not-Pure-Being (that is, nothingness). In creating the universe, God makes a voluntary dilution of his own perfect existence, and a mathematically perfect computation of the most perfect binary number, where one equals being and zero equals nothingness. This creation is bound to produce evil in the following classes:

- Metaphysical Evil, or limitation (which is therefore necessary for all components of the universe which are not God);
- Moral Evil, or sin;
- Physical Evil, or pain.

Metaphysical evil is the fundamental evil, from which moral and physical evils naturally and unavoidably flow. Metaphysical evil is obviously negative, a *privatio boni*. The moral and physical evils which flow from it are also therefore intrinsically negative. God's unavoidable inclusion of non-being in the universe explains its lack of perfection.

While there are clear problems with Leibniz's account,[19] he remained wedded to his characterizing of the universe as formed in binary configuration in order to combine the Principle of Sufficient Reason and the Principle of the Best to yield the Best Possible World. The Principle of Sufficient Reason – very simply a basic and uncontentious premise of empirical science, that no event occurs without a cause sufficient to explain its occurrence – will propel scientific explanations for the existence of the universe towards an overarching metaphysical explanation of why the universe we experience is this particular one rather than one of the infinitely-large other possible universes.[20] The Principle of the Best is the application of the Principle of Sufficient

Reason to contingent truths under a criterion of divine perfection to produce the Best Possible World.

Lest we worry that Leibniz is guilty here of compounding too many extravagant metaphysical principles, his underlying point is simply that theism involves God's creation of the universe being *motivated*, and not just being a random act of will. So God's choosing among an infinity of possibilities involves a rational and perfect application of judgement. Consequently, the Sufficient Reason for a universe brought into being by God, rather than a purposeless, randomly existing universe, is bound to result in the Best Possible World.

This link between the Principle of Sufficient Reason and the Principle of the Best, grounded in God's motives for creating the universe, is essential to Leibniz's theodicy. Without it, the Principle of Sufficient Reason applied to phenomena in the world yields only the truth that this universe is logically determined in a certain way, which is trivially true. To make this 'certain' way equal a 'good' way, rather than an 'entirely morally indifferent' way, a theistic Principle of the *Best* is needed.

The Principle of Sufficient Reason on its own is a highly persuasive hypothesis, with considerable teleological and psychological force. But to employ it is to place Leibniz's theodicy on the firmly *a posteriori* territory of a psychological analogy between 'the nature of individuals' interdependence indicating a universal harmony' and 'God'. And, to come full circle, this empirically produced argument has a major empirical weakness – the Problem of Evil.

Leibniz, in attempting to argue not just *a posteriori* but *a priori* for the Best Possible World, postulates the necessary existence of a Perfect Being.[21] Leibniz's argument is essentially to assert that all perfect attributes are logically compossible and compatible because they are simple. But this is a hypothesis, not a proof; and this non-proof leaves Leibniz in insuperable difficulties in his search for an *a priori* theodicy. His metaphysics are divorced from his logic, and become an interesting but logically uncompelling hypothetical structure.

Nonetheless, Leibniz's Best Possible World, even if only an *a posteriori* hypothesis reliant on the Principle of Sufficient Reason, encourages theology to keep pace with the sciences, with the aim of producing a description of evil and its origins and cures which reaches beyond our own experience and is rooted in the divine motives for creating the universe. This step beyond human history into cosmology is not deistic, because Leibniz's appeal to the Principle of the Best must be actively theistic, involving as it does a Principle of the Best rather than a Principle of Indifference. It therefore points towards a religious faith and not just towards a conventional scientific trust in the Principle of Sufficient Reason.

One uneasiness arising from this theodicy centres on its programmatic character. For Leibniz there undoubtedly was evil in the world, but all of it stemmed from the metaphysically essential distinction of the perfect God from his creation which, not being God, was therefore less than perfect and suffered from limitation and its consequences. But for Leibniz, the normal theistic argument that in at least one possible world there is a balance of good over evil does not have to be shown, because (given his metaphysical presuppositions) if there exists anything at all, it *a priori* has to be ultimately positive. Leibniz's Optimism becomes almost vacuous when one considers that the Best Possible World is consistent with the universe being principally *bad*. All Leibniz has to claim is that all other possible worlds must in principle be worse.

What are we to make of this cheery excursus into eighteenth-century philosophy of religion? We have seen that Leibniz is notable for his failure to give an account of an *a priori* proof of the existence of God, but what remains is an ingenious *a posteriori* argument, which amounts to an intricate cosmological myth of Optimism.

If Christian choosing involves a leap of faith, then we might argue that Leibniz's incorrigible faith in Optimism offers a more palatable and reasonable initial foundation for theism than faith in the Pessimism of the Fall. However, while in this way aesthetically superior to Pessimism, Optimism still falls short as a coherent and reasonable theodicy because the programmatic nature of its claims – that whatever ills occur in the universe, it must still by definition be the Best Possible World – renders irrelevant any *ethical* attempts to address the Mystery of Evil. This makes Optimism less morally offensive than Pessimism, but still so passive and complacent as readily to fall within the critical ambit even of the soft materialist, who wonders what serious moral difference theism would by definition make to the world.

Fleshing out a Theodicy in a Historical Evolutionary Ethics: Why We Act Against Evil

We have seen that Leibniz's programmatic formalism is an inadequate theodicy because it is empirically and personally detached in ways which divorce theism of moral (but not of metaphysical) seriousness: it appears to be an exposition of theism which fails to address why thinking and feeling human beings behave in the ways which they actually do to counteract evil.

Normal theism has an ineluctable ethical dimension, which Optimism of Leibniz's type makes irrelevant and unnecessary. So the theist requires not just the supportive and hopeful foundational *metaphysic* of Optimism, but an additional religious *narrative* which accounts for human behaviour being conducted as if Optimism were not true – because if Optimism were strictly and completely true, we would seem to have no moral need to bother acting against evil.

J. S. Mill argued that, even if theism is true, our moral judgements about the necessity of stopping evil are inconsistent with our truly believing its truth.[22] Consider the following. If we *really* trusted that God exists and that all is for the best in the Best Possible World; or even, failing Leibniz's programmatic absolute Optimism, that all evil is at least redeemable and will be redeemed by a loving God, then we would have no moral need to lift a finger to save a drowning child, because if the ultimate consequences would be better if the child dies, then the death is a net good, and if the consequences would be worse if the child dies, then God will ensure that in fact she lives. So the fact that we regularly and as a matter of the strongest moral conviction act to save children from drowning and strenuously to prevent the occurrence of other evils mitigates against our theistic claims of profound trust in the existence of God.

The theist replies that even if we sincerely believed that there is a God who ultimately redeems all unnecessary evil, but that we weren't quite sure of it, then we would still be under an obligation to prevent whatever evil we could: if God exists, there are no grave eternal consequences if I intervene to save the drowning child or not. If God does not exist, there are no grave eternal consequences if I intervene, but dreadful consequences if I don't; so I should intervene. Even if this answer subordinates our confidence in the truth of theism to our confidence in our common moral sensibilities, the theist might still argue that the lack of certainty in the truth of theism implied by this common moral approach is part of the essential calculus of modern theistic belief, where the truth of God's benevolent existence is of course anything but certain.

Even if our saving the drowning child demonstrates that our ethics override our theism for practical purposes, this does not diminish the parallel metaphysical attractiveness of theism. However confident our ethical standpoints, a metaphysical supplement seems required to satisfy our craving for answers to the huge personal questions of life, not least to the Problem of Evil. It is therefore quite consistent to save the drowning child as a theist, because the lack of guarantee of theism's truth legitimately allows us to hedge our bets by acting in every case against evil. We might nonetheless reasonably hope and trust that a theistic metaphysical Optimism is true even as we save the drowning child, and we might correctly try to marshal *a posteriori* arguments for it.

Moving from general metaphysical to overtly religious categories, we might add that Pessimism does not agree (whereas Optimism is entirely consistent) with what John Hick (1985) calls the 'minority report' in Christian theology, namely an Irenaean theodicy, according to which exponents of the lapsarian view are looking in the wrong direction. The Fall looks backwards in time to find an explanation for human suffering, and finds it by interpreting Genesis 3 in certain ways which we have seen are morally deficient. But for Irenaeus of Lyons and his followers, interpreting Genesis 1, the answer to human suffering lies in the future, in God's eschatological fulfilment of all creation.[23] God has deliberately created an initially imperfect universe in order that those made in his image may evolve, develop and work towards being fashioned too in his likeness. (Here Irenaeus shows himself every bit as much an imperfect exegete of Genesis 1:26 as Augustine is of Genesis 3!)

According to this religious and ethical framework, the purpose of God's creation of mankind is that, sharing God's image, we are blessed with the faculty of free choice, and capable of using this aright or of abusing it. The end result of our learning through trial and error to use our choices for the good is better than our being dumb, thoughtless automata programmed in advance to behave well. This world of human free will is the Best Possible World, and its supreme effect – a world in which other minds might exist alongside God as sharing his freedom of informed, benevolent, wise choice – is unobtainable in any other way.

This free will defence, according to which a world of free agents is intrinsically better and more desirable than a world of morally frictionless automata, is grounded in moral sentiments about the superiority of autonomy, freedom and democracy to oppression, tyranny and bullying which run deeper than any other human notions. It involves a theistic account of God deliberately relinquishing a part of his omnipotence by choosing to create a type of being which has separate free will. God relinquishes his omnipotence in creating mankind because not even an omnipotent being can ensure that someone freely does an action rather than an imagined alternative action.[24]

The raw account here is of a God who thus takes a risk. He decides to create beings with free will who are perfectly capable of performing acts of breathtaking evil, but who need not do this, and who are indeed capable of performing acts of great love and care instead. That this universe is ultimately the Best Possible World involves God inviting humanity to collaborate with him in developing the world for good and in combatting evil, such that for any given instance of potential evil, God hopes that the individual concerned will act to prevent that evil. If the individual fails to act to prevent the evil, it may or may not be the case that God will intervene anyway. However, it will probably be the case that God will not intervene in any way more direct than via the general physical laws. So it is mankind's responsibility to act to prevent evil and maximize good as far as possible. God trusts human beings to do this, but there is no guarantee that we will comply with God's hopes, and God's risk may in many instances prove a failure. Outstanding examples of human failure include Auschwitz. In parallel, theists continue to trust that the evils consequent to these failures will be redeemed, although the particular eschatological manner in which this aspect of the Best Possible World will unfold remains wholly obscure.

This free will account accords with our best ideals of ethical behaviour, which is practically impatient with the logical theodicy that all evils are necessary. We endorse popular laws prohibiting murder and rape, and our daily moral judgements are based in this way on considerations which are not absolutely theistic. But this paradox is – even for the theist – essential to a theistic way of seeing the world and doing things in it. Our lack of any guarantee of the truth of theism compels us to make daily judgements and laws based on the premise that there is no God, or at any rate no God who is active. I see someone about to commit a murder and (as a theist too) I do all in my power to prevent them. This materially implies that I take that at least some evil to be unnecessary. But our ethics are still most effective, the theist claims, when grounded in a theistic metaphysics. And the theist holds that a world in which there is the opportunity for people to intervene to prevent evil is morally superior to a world in which there is no possibility to prevent evil.[25] This ethical theism asserts that it is better for me to prevent an evil act than for God to prevent it, because it is on the whole not good for God directly to violate the usual course of the laws of physics.

Such a defence of ethical development is not an exhaustive theodicy – it does not begin to make the bold *a priori* claims which Leibniz postulated. It only aims to say that, to take a monstrous example, the vileness of Auschwitz is not inconsistent with the existence of a good God, who in creating the universe has two choices:

- a world of significant freedom including a contingently un-avoidable Auschwitz;
- a not-Auschwitz world of benign human automata who lack the essential human freedom to commit grotesque evil.

If God elects to create the first of these worlds, various evils are avoidable from the human point of view, but unavoidable from God's point of view. In short, God could not guarantee a not-Auschwitz world at the point of creation without things *in toto* being worse. So while things are worse as a result of Auschwitz, and things would have been better if men had prevented it, things would have been even worse if God had intervened to prevent it.

Combining a Developing Human Ethics and a Metaphysical Optimism: Active Optimism

We have seen that for all practical purposes, a view of progress which sees humanity developing into the moral likeness of God and struggling to do what is right and to cooperate with God in combatting evil is the best available religious narrative for the theist in addressing the Problem of Evil. This day-to-day ethical action could in theory be grounded either in the theological Pessimism or Optimism described above. While accepting that either move is possible, I hold that the overwhelmingly more intelligent theistic move is to link this active ethic of develop-ment with a metaphysical Optimism.

The excuse for indulging in this sort of theoretical talk lies both in doing it on behalf of an organization which actually grapples with Mystery of Evil, and also in seeing that many of the other debates which the Church conducts (such as move-ments about the interpretation of the Bible, about liturgy and in

101

favour of ecumenism) are predicated on the trustworthiness of the basic ethical currency of theism, and rely on its truth.

Theists must think about and discuss the Problem of Evil precisely because theism lacks guarantees of its own truth. The consequent free debate allows the theist to attempt to persuade him or herself and others towards Optimism. On the other hand, a materialist account of evil, lacking the metaphysical underpinning of theism, lacking theism's eschatological vision, lacking theism's dogged insistence on a perfect ultimate justice, and not necessarily wedded to theism's core doctrine of the dignity of individual human freedom and choice, quickly reduces itself to a hopeless, unimaginative and limited vision, offering neither comfort nor interpretative value. To that materialism, a theism grounded in Optimism and eager to work out a developing ethics is able to ask, What is the point of the universe? Materialism's answers (insofar as there are any) have persistently seemed intuitively untrue to the clear majority of human beings across the ages and cultures, and both before and after the Enlightenment.

For a mixture of historical reasons, the Church of England is well placed determinedly to address the Mystery of Evil, as well as to continue to think freely and honestly about the Problem of Evil.

A Monotheistic Coda

The reader will have noticed that the suggestions for debate which we have examined in this chapter are not limited to a Christian analysis. I have deliberately used 'Christian' and 'theist' as interchangeably and untidily as possible. The theistic defence of Optimism and evolutionary ethics outlined above would seem to be equally applicable in some Jewish and Muslim theologies.

For me, the best approach to the Problem of Evil is not to rest on the illusory security of key religious jargons, but to cast the terms of reflection as broadly and deeply as possible. The fundamental issue is the meaning and purpose of human existence in the light of our suffering, and not the future of any particular cultural manifestation of the religious impulse. If I have, as a priest of the Church of England, the total freedom to express arguments in favour of a general and authentic theistic solution to the Problem, that is all to the favour of the inclusive openness of my Church.

Answers in theodicy are more than just Christian – after Leibniz, solutions have been sought which are not too obviously mythological. Again after Leibniz's logical failures, metaphysics might have to abandon its quest for *a priori* proofs of God – and the existence of evil seems a physical fact sufficiently heavy to force theology to conduct its arguments *a posteriori* and with a humility which operates through persuasion rather than submission.

Once any theist has reflected enough to reject an intellectual method of theocracy (grounded in submission to particular revealed Scriptures which must compete with other allegedly revealed Scriptures) in favour of an intellectual method of persuasion (grounded in an adherence to reason which can command common assent), the way is clear to articulating a solution to the Problem of Evil which is capable of appealing to anyone who is dissatisfied with the explanatory limitations and personal unimaginativeness of materialism. Active Optimism is an attempt at such a solution.

We may now see that this sophisticated, supple theodicy, allied to firm pastoral action, is the best answer to the soft atheist and the hard materialist in facing the Problem of Evil. Active Optimism is *par excellence* the Anglican way.

Notes

1   See, for example, Neiman (2002). Subtitling her book 'An Alternative History of Philosophy', Neiman reinterprets the whole of post-Enlightenment Western philosophy as a response to the Problem of Evil
2   See Hick (1985), Chapter 1.2.
3   See pp. 49–50.
4   According to the Research and Statistics Dept of the Archbishops' Council of the Church of England, 232,560 funerals were conducted by Anglican ministers in England in 2000 (105,250 in churches and 127,310 in crematoria). According to the Office of National Statistics, 500,959 people died in England in 2000. See www.cofe.anglican.org.
5   See McCabe (1981), p. 6.
6   See Leibniz (1985), para. 21.
7   See Van Inwagen (1988).
8   Leibniz (1985), Preliminary dissertation on the conformity of faith with reason, para. 60.
9   See Sextus Empiricus (1996), pp. 173–5.
10 See Mackie (1955).
11 See Swinburne (1977), Chapter 4.
12 Dostoyevsky (1982), V, 4.
13 This is his thesis in Swinburne (1998).
14 See Phillips (1986), Chapter 4, where Phillips explicitly opposes Swinburne.
15 See Sölle (2001), p. 64. Larrimore's reader offers an excellent and broad introduction to and overview of the Problem of Evil.
16 See Augustine of Hippo (1998), XIV. Augustine's doctrine of free will, involving the exercise of choice, is one which I support in this chapter. It is his account of the historical importance of the Fall which argues with modern sensibility and science.
17 See Ezekiel 28:12–19, 2 Peter 2:4 and Jude 6. For vaguer accounts, see Isaiah 14:12–15 and Revelation 12:4–9.
18 Leibniz (1985) contains all the arguments which follow.
19 We may immediately point out a handful of philosophical problems. Leibniz does not show the mechanism whereby moral and physical evils flow from metaphysical evil, nor does he show whether metaphysical evil will necessarily produce moral and physical evils. Nor does he show that if metaphysical evil is negative, and if moral and physical evils flow from metaphysical evil, that it logically follows that moral and physical evils are

therefore negative. More basically, Leibniz does not explain why this alleged pure negativity of evil is true when it is so counter-intuitive – evils are not experienced by us as negative. More basically still, Leibniz does not explain why he can reliably hold that good and evil are simple binary opposites, and that good is the 'better' and more positive of them. See Broad (1975), Chapter 7.

20 Despite seeming intuitively true, the Principle of Sufficient Reason is disputed. See Rowe (1975), p. 85f.

21 René Descartes had shown to his satisfaction in his third *Meditation* that if the idea of a Perfect Being was possible, it exists. But he had not shown that the idea was possible in ways which go beyond pseudo-idea musings about 'the greatest natural number' or 'the largest circle'. Leibniz attempted to fill the gaps in Descartes' argument. See Leibniz (1996), IV, para. 7f.

22 Mill (1969) especially 'The utility of religion'.

23 Irenaeus of Lyons (1992), IV.

24 J. L. Mackie has challenged this proposition: since it is perfectly possible for me on a single occasion to choose freely to do a good action rather than an evil action, then it is logically possible for all my actions to be freely chosen and to be good rather than evil, see Mackie (1955 B.4). In reply, the theist might argue that there is indeed a logically possible world in which God creates free creatures who happen to choose good freely. But it would be contingently unavoidable for evil to enter such a world – and if evil did not enter it, this would be due to metaphysical chance.

25 This is a delicately balanced view, because no theist would extrapolate from this to the supplementary position that we should attempt to commit evil in order to give others the opportunity to prevent these evils coming to pass.

References

Augustine of Hippo ([413] 1998) *The City of God against the Pagans* (trans. R. W. Dyson). Cambridge: Cambridge University Press.

Broad, C. D. (1975) *Leibniz* (ed. C. Lewy). Cambridge: Cambridge University Press.

Dostoyevsky, F. M. ([1880] 1982) *The Brothers Karamazov* (trans. D. Magarshack). Harmondsworth: Penguin Books.

Hick, J. (1985) *Evil and the God of Love* (2nd edn, revised). London: Macmillan Press.

Irenaeus of Lyons ([2nd century CE] 1992) *Against the Heresies* (trans. D. J. Unger, rev. J. J. Dillon). New York: Paulist Press.

Leibniz, G. W. ([1710] 1985) *Theodicy: Essays on the Goodness of God, the Freedom of Man and the Origin of Evil* (ed. A. Farrer, trans. E. M. Huggard). La Salle, IL: Open Court Press.

Leibniz, G. W. ([1765] 1996) *New Essays on Human Understanding* (trans. and ed. P. Remnant and J. Bennett). Cambridge: Cambridge University Press.

McCabe, H. (1981) 'Evil', *New Blackfriars*, 62, 4–17.

Mackie, J. L. (1955) 'Evil and omnipotence', *Mind*, 64, 200–12.

Mill, J. S. ([1874] 1969) 'Three essays on religion', in J. M. Robson (ed.), *The Collected Works of John Stuart Mill*. Toronto: University of Toronto Press, X.

Neiman, S. (2002) *Evil in Modern Thought*. Princeton, NJ: Princeton University Press.

Phillips, D. Z. (1986) *Belief, Change and Forms of Life*. London: Macmillan.

Rowe, W. L. (1975) 'The cosmological argument and the principle of sufficient reason', in W. L. Rowe, *The Cosmological Argument*. Princeton, NJ: Princeton University Press, pp. 60–114.

Sextus Empiricus ([*c*.200 CE] 1996), 'Outlines of Pyrrhonism', III, 3, in Benson Mates (trans.) *The Skeptic Way: Sextus Empiricus's Outlines of Pyrrhonism*. New York: Oxford University Press.

Sölle, D. ([1975] 2001) 'A critique of Christian masochism', in M. J. Larrimore (ed.), *The Problem of Evil: A Reader*. Oxford: Blackwell Publishers.

Swinburne, R. (1977) 'The problem of evil', in S. C. Brown (ed.), *Reason and Religion*. Ithaca, NY: Cornell University Press.

Swinburne, R. (1998) *Providence and the Problem of Evil*. Oxford: Oxford University Press.

Van Inwagen, P. (1988) 'The magnitude, duration and distribution of evil: a theodicy', *Philosophical Topics*, 16, 2: 161–87.

Part III

Engagement

5

Issues of Life and Death: Why Medical Ethics Needs the Church

Jeremy Caddick

Introduction

Nowadays issues in medical ethics are rarely out of the newspapers or out of the courts. We begin with two such cases. In September 2002 Natallie Evans and Lorraine Hadley went to the High Court in an attempt to prevent the destruction of embryos created with their eggs and with sperm from partners with whom they have now split up. The current state of the law requires the consent of both gamete providers if such embryos are to be stored or to be used, either for treatment or research. If the absence of such consent the embryos must, in the words of the 1990 Human Fertilisation and Embryology Act, be 'allowed to perish'. The Act allows those whose eggs or sperm are stored to vary or withdraw their consent at any time before the embryo is placed in a woman.

It was reported that the partners of the two women were reluctant to allow the birth of children for whom they might be financially responsible. The women concerned have been suffering from medical conditions that mean they will be unable to produce any more eggs. These embryos thus represent their last chance of having a child that is genetically theirs.

The women do not contest the fact that the 1990 Act gives their former partners a veto over the continued storage or use of the embryos. They argue that this provision breaches their human rights. Speaking to the BBC, their lawyer said that the women 'argue that it's unfair that their former partners have that veto, and they use the analogy that if they got pregnant naturally and the embryos were in their bodies, then their respective partners would not have any say at all'.[1]

They are able to mount such an action because of the passage of the Human Rights Act 1998, which has incorporated the European Convention on Human Rights directly into British Law. The framework of the Convention will almost certainly give rise to many cases such as that of Ms Hadley and Ms Evans which test the current regulatory framework governing fertility treatment. In particular the provisions of Article 12 which protects 'the right to marry and found a family' and of Article 14 which prohibits discrimination, are likely to be extensively argued over.

Lawyers for the two women seek to draw an analogy between their situation and what would be the case if they were able to have children naturally. This is a move that is frequently made in the debate over the regulation of fertility treatment and new reproductive technologies. Appeal is frequently made to the fact that the having of children outside fertility clinics is not regulated at all and that those who are able to become pregnant without the assistance of such medical technology face no restrictions. What then is the justification for restricting people's choice if they are unfortunate enough to be less fertile than others? Appeals to reproductive liberty are used to argue that the people should be allowed to take full advantage of the possibilities opened up by advances in technology, subject (usually) to the proviso that they do not harm others.

The fact of disputes such as those between Ms Hadley, Ms Evans and their former partners is itself a partial answer to such questions. A framework is needed to adjudicate when people fall out over the use of this technology. However, the deeper question remains. What limits (if any) should be placed on the ways in which people may have children? Single women and lesbian couples are currently treated at some, but not all, fertility clinics in the UK. Treatment of women substantially past menopausal age is frowned upon and reproductive cloning is both technologically impractical and unlawful.

The second case is that of Dianne Pretty, which turned on her claim that she had a right to die. Her application under the same Convention was turned down by the European Court of Human Rights in April 2002, having been similarly rejected by the courts up to and including the House of Lords in the UK.

Mrs Pretty was suffering from Motor Neurone Disease and eventually died as a result of the disease a matter of days after the European Court had given its judgment. She went to court seeking a declaration that the prohibition on assisting suicide contained in the Suicide Act of 1961 conflicted with her rights under the European Convention. What she wanted was an assurance that her husband would not be prosecuted if he helped her kill herself. She appealed to several of the rights mentioned in the convention, but most notably to Article 2, the right to life. Her lawyers argued that the right to life includes a right to decide when one's life should end. The judges comprehensively disagreed, holding that a right to die would be the antithesis of a right to life, not a corollary of it. They pointed to the wording of the relevant article, 'Everyone's life shall be protected by law. No one shall be deprived of his life intentionally.' What Mrs Pretty was asking for was permission precisely that her life be intentionally ended.

Both of these cases involve arguments about rights. There are, of course, perfectly sufficient legal explanations for this. The passage of the Human Rights Act made it virtually inevitable that there would be a rash of cases that challenged the UK law on human rights grounds. In both cases what the applicants are claiming is not that the UK law is being interpreted wrongly –

the provisions of both the Suicide Act 1961 and the Human Fertilisation and Embryology Act 1990 are, in each case, clear – but rather that these provisions conflict with the human rights of those concerned. We will consider the two cases in more detail later, but behind the legal developments that give rise to this sort of case there stands a growth, not to say an already established dominance, of the language of rights as the framework for dealing with ethical issues. I wish to point out that there are drawbacks to such a rights-dominated approach. In particular, though, I wish to draw attention to the way that the Church is well placed, perhaps uniquely well placed, to make up some of the deficiencies of a rights-based approach to ethics. In short, the language of rights and its consequent attention to the importance of choice and decision-making will always require an account of what things are good to choose and what things are bad. The framework of rights is, by itself, too insubstantial to guide us.

Formally speaking, a framework of rights should serve to make space for people freely to select the conceptions of what constitutes a good life. In a pluralist society such as ours, the argument goes, there will be a variety of conceptions of the human good on offer. What constructions such as the European Convention on Human Rights or the US Constitution do is, as it were, hold the ring between these competing conceptions. It is up to individuals to choose the code by which they live.

If we are to lead good lives, we certainly have to have the freedom to make the choices that are necessary to that. However, there is more to making good choices than the freedom of the decision-making process itself. One of the dangers of a rights-based approach is that we come to think that the fact that something is chosen by itself makes it good.

It will be argued that in practice what we see is not a robust debate between different conceptions of the good life, but rather a squabbling over rights and their limits, as evidenced in the

cases mentioned above. Something more is needed, some resources of wisdom that will allow people to engage with what it
is that makes life good, so that their choosing, and the constraints that are put on their choosing, are not simply about the
satisfying of personal preferences but about the quest to find
what is worthwhile in human living.

The Church has such resources of wisdom, as do other,
non-Christian, religious traditions.[2] In principle, there can, and
should, be many others. They seem, however, at least in terms
of the public debate as it is carried on today in the supposedly
secular West to be less in evidence.

The Church's account of what is good in and for human life
will be formed by its account of the paradigmatic human life,
that of Jesus the Christ. The Church approaches the world in
which we live as the gift of a beneficent creator. These two facts
will always act to resist the sterile reductivism that seems to be
a mark of so much secular ethics. We cannot be reduced to mere
choosing agents who make ourselves by imposing our will on
the neutral stuff of the world if we are creatures, made in the
image of our creator and potentially brothers and sisters of the
risen and glorified Son.

In what follows we will examine these two cases further to
see how this works in practice, how secular medical ethics, if it
is not to become sterile draws (often without acknowledgement)
on the richer account of our humanity that is contained in the
Church's tradition.

This opens up possibilities for dialogue, or more properly for
mission, so long as we rigorously exclude any coercive or
triumphalist elements of that term. It is not, after all, the case
that Christian ethics applies only to Christians (even if many
secular moral philosophers would like to imply that it is so). The
human existence we are discussing is the existence that is common to all humans. Its contours are not the product of our free

and unfettered choice, but of a complex interplay of the biological facts of our physical being, our psychological equipment and our cultural backgrounds, as well as of the effects of our individual wills interacting with the world around us. We are therefore able to share the resources that our tradition contains with those who do not identify themselves as Christians. We do so in the expectation that our experience will be recognized as informing theirs. Such wells of wisdom are necessary to provide the fuel to drive the engine of ethical deliberation.

The possibility of such sharing of wisdom often turns on things as apparently superficial as the tone of voice and attitude to the other. It does not imply any weakening of belief or hesitancy about what Christianity has to say about human existence. The reverse would be closer to the truth. Ethics can be dogmatic, in the sense that, for example, Michael Banner uses the term,[3] without having to be expressed dogmatically. Indeed, Banner takes issue with precisely the assumption that if ethics is dogmatic it is thereby sectarian and inward-looking.

The title of this chapter is a deliberate echoing of that of a much reprinted paper by Stanley Hauerwas.[4] There he argues that the Church is uniquely able to support medicine, since the vocation of those who practise medicine involves being present with those who are suffering. The Church is a community which has a particular role in overcoming the divisive effects of pain, and being present for those who suffer. 'Only a people trained in remembering, and in remembering as a communal act, their sins and pains can offer a paradigm for sustaining across time a painful memory so that it acts to heal rather than to divide.'[5]

Rights and their Limitations

Before considering our two cases in more detail it is probably worth making some general comments about the language of rights and its drawbacks. One clearly has to be extremely circumspect here. The language of rights is appealing, in part, because the opposites – coercion, oppression, exploitation – are so obviously and so egregiously bad.

Alasdair MacIntyre[6] explicitly makes the link between rights and struggles against oppression, exploitation and coercion. The language of rights is unavoidably the language of protest, of claiming something from others who are (allegedly) unjustly withholding it. The history of the concept of rights shows just how effective it is for this purpose. However protest, even justified protest against a manifest evil, remains just that. It is not communication; it is struggle. MacIntyre thus sees rights as a symptom of the moral collapse to which he seeks to draw our attention.[7]

Rights are linked to the exercise of autonomy. Some accounts of rights will make this link explicitly and claim that the possession of autonomy is a necessary condition for the possession of rights. That is, rights are about *choosing* things and an ability to choose is therefore a precondition of having a right.

Other more thoughtful philosophers[8] see that this does not accord with our actual practice with regard to rights since we see no logical problem in according legal rights to non-autonomous beings such as very young children or animals. Someone can without contradiction, for example, leave a sum of money after their death to an infant or a pet. The *right* of the infant or pet to the money can be coherently defended against those who would wish to deprive them of it.

Such an approach will identify *interests* rather than autonomy as the basis of rights; whether something can be benefited or harmed is the logical precondition of having a right. We cannot, for example, coherently speak of *harming* a piece of rock.

There are two comments to be made about this line of thought. First, it does not break the link with autonomy and the exercise of choice, since someone who is capable of exercising their autonomy by asserting a right that they have is closer to the logical centre of the concept of a right than a non-autonomous individual who requires another to act on their behalf.

Second, even an interest-based approach sets a standard for moral considerability. Objects or beings that, as it were, fail the test, do not carry moral weight. For example the interest approach is developed by Bonnie Steinbock[9] and applied to questions surrounding the unborn. Sentience, she argues, following Feinberg, is necessary to having interests since one cannot be benefited or harmed without at least some rudimentary cognitive equipment with which to be aware of it. Sentience, rather than autonomy, is thus the test for moral status. The pre-sentient foetus fails the test, and therefore abortion before this point is not a harm to the foetus (though it may be to the mother or others who are sentient).

This is thus the first drawback of a rights-based approach, that there will always be those who do not possess the required capabilities to qualify as rightholders. If autonomy is the basis of rights then those who are not autonomous – the very young, the very old and the severely handicapped, for example – will enter a grey area in which their moral status is not directly accorded, but is dependent on the concern that others, who are autonomous, feel for them.

The problem remains even if we adopt an interest-based rather than an autonomy-based account of rights, since the pass mark is now not being autonomous, but being sentient. There are still, however, human lives that do not make the grade, whom we might have cause to think should not be dismissed so lightly. The sentience criterion excludes not only the pre-sentient foetus, as we have seen, but also the comatose and those in a persistent vegetative state (PVS).

Peter Singer, a leading secular writer on ethics (though more accurately identified with a utilitarian approach than a rights-based one), is unapologetic about his attachment to sentience as marking the boundary of moral considerability. Famously he sees nothing inherently wrong with the killing of pre-autonomous newborns (for example, handicapped babies), if doing so would increase the total amount of happiness in the world.[10] When challenged on the issue of whether his utilitarian philosophy disadvantages those who are not sentient, he replies chillingly, 'Utilitarianism does not so much exclude the non-sentient from equal consideration of interests, *as they find that they have no interests to consider.*'[11]

The Beginning of Life

Natallie Evans and Lorraine Hadley claim that the current state of the law infringes their human rights. Were they to become pregnant against the wishes of their former partners, then those partners would, we can assume, be making a similar claim about their human rights.

The two women are very likely to lose their case because the current law is framed with more than half an eye on avoiding precisely such disputes. The creation, storage and use of embryos are sanctioned by the Human Fertilisation and Embryology Act for as long as all the parties are in agreement. Without such agreement, like some stern parent, the law simply declares the game to be over and sends everyone home; the embryos are 'allowed to perish'.

The women's lawyers' contention that they are being discriminated against in that if they were not infertile the embryos would have been created inside their wombs rather than in a laboratory and would therefore be protected from destruction, whatever their partner's wish, is unlikely to impress the court either. Courts have resolutely refused to grant fathers any say at all in decisions over abortion and even refuse to sanction interventions necessary to safeguard the health of a near-term foetus.[12] In such cases the courts again take a pragmatic approach, refusing to be drawn into arguments over embryos and foetuses (which do not achieve legal personality until birth). The law will, however, bestir itself to protect bodily integrity by refusing to countenance the physical coercion of the women concerned. This is the legal reason that the women's analogy with the situation that would pertain if their embryos had been created without the aid of IVF does not lead to the conclusion they desire. The fathers would not have a veto over the embryos' continued growth because any such power would compromise the bodily integrity of the women.

The passage of the Human Rights Act thus gives the women a chance to re-open an issue that would otherwise have been closed, but the framework of rights in itself does not obviously help to resolve the dispute.

The having of children is one area in which the limitations of the language of rights and autonomy are particularly clear. The addition of the phrase 'designer babies' (whether appropriate or not) to news stories about pre-implantation genetic diagnosis, or gene therapy, acts as a signpost warning us to be cautious. The possible production of 'designer babies' is taken to be self-evidently something to be avoided, since we all know, don't we, that babies are not like washing machines or cars or clothes. It is indeed true that babies are not like consumer durables, and it is also true that most people react with horror to any suggestion that they should be treated as if they were. It is less clear why, from a rights-based point of view, this should be so.

The advocates of procreative liberty[13] are not slow to apply the rhetoric and the logic of rights to our decisions about reproduction. Why, subject only to the condition of not harming others, should people not be allowed to use medical technology to have children in whatever way they choose? Such rhetorical questions are usually accompanied by the observation that IVF and other forms of fertility treatment are more tightly regulated than natural parenting.

The obvious response to this last point is that the facts of biology place constraints on the ways in which people can have children. New reproductive technologies allow us to overcome these constraints, both involving many more parties in the process (gamete donors, surrogate parents, etc.) and allowing intervention over a longer period (for example, while gametes or embryos are stored). These possibilities in themselves are reason to exercise caution.

However, the deeper problem with such reproductive libertarianism is the wholesale inappropriateness of trying to say anything very meaningful about families and family relationships in terms of rights, autonomy and choice.

Perhaps the single most significant feature of family relationships is that they *do not* rest on choice. We do not choose most of the members of our family. We don't choose who our parents are. We do not have a contract with our children. Nor do we choose our siblings. Superficially it may look as if we do choose our spouse or partner, but the more you look at that relationship, the less satisfactory a choice-based account of it becomes.

Because they are not based on choice, family relationships challenge this dominant way of thinking. This clash has a whole host of deleterious consequences for family life and the way we view it. First of all, it makes it quite simply invisible. When we assess our lives in terms of the choices that we have made, our family relationships simply don't come up on the screen. Second, if choice is the only category we have, the only shot in our locker, we will grievously mistreat our family relationships when we try to pay them attention, when, for example, they are going badly. 'I wasn't given a choice about having you as my parent' becomes an accusation, when it should be a simple statement of fact. Trying to force family relationships into the straitjacket of 'choice' mangles and distorts them.

Children are the physical embodiment of the self-giving (on both sides) that a sexual relationship involves. The commitment involved in having children is total and open-ended. It is the complete opposite of a contract or an agreement. There are no clauses limiting the number of times that a child can wake up in the middle of the night, no limit to how naughty they can be at school. They are, and remain, your children.

That there are drawbacks to approaching questions about parenthood using the language of rights is apparent to many, whether they share an explicitly Christian outlook or not. Onora O'Neill,[14] for example, criticizes the use of autonomy-based arguments on the grounds that the dependence of children will limit the autonomy of parents in ways that cannot be predicted, and criticizes the individual focus of rights as inappropriate to questions of reproduction because parenthood is inherently and obviously not the act of a single individual.

Thus we see the same pattern repeating itself. The language of rights and autonomy does not capture our practice or our moral experience. In this case families and parenting are just not subject to choice and agreement in the way that the framework of rights would suggest. But why are families not like that? A religious approach will give an account that is based on our relationship with God. It is difficult to see what a purely secular approach would have to offer that was at all comparable.

It is no accident that we talk about God as our *parent*. The same unconditional self-giving is seen in his relationship with us, the same patience, the same determination not to give up on us.

In a biblical context we can see this most clearly through the concept of a covenant. Like a marriage, a covenant may superficially look like an agreement. A closer examination, however, reveals something different and more significant. The OT is the story of God's efforts to make a covenant relationship with his people. With Noah, with Moses, with Abraham with David, God makes and remakes his covenant. It is grounded, not in consent, but in God's promises to his people. His promise to Abraham is fundamental to the OT story. He promises that Abraham will be the father of many nations and he promises to give him the land of Canaan. What is required of Abraham is simply faithfulness. Through the OT the relationship needs to be remade repeatedly because even that is too much to ask. Finally, the relationship is remade in Jesus, the *New* Covenant, that is the basis of the Christian faith.

At its most fundamental a covenant relationship is not based on anything resembling choice, but on God's solemn declaration, 'I am God Almighty; walk before me, and be blameless. And I will make my covenant between me and you, and will make you exceedingly numerous.'[15]

Family relationships are best understood therefore, as examples of *covenant* relationships. That is what is special about them and also what is most commonly overlooked. The covenant relationship that we have with our children is grounded in the covenant relationship between their parents, which is in turn grounded in the covenant relationship with God.

Thus, we can see that there is positive value in having children, and therefore a positive value in the advances in medical technology that make it possible for many for whom it was previously not so.

The language of rights fails such people. It reduces their desire for children to a lifestyle choice, because it has no other category in which to place it. Childlessness becomes a tragedy because such people *want* children very much. It is the strength of their frustrated desire that comes to the fore, rather than the substantive importance of having children. For the same reason

121

the question of *why* people want children remains opaque. If asked at all, it is attributed to 'biology' or to what is 'natural', as if the givenness of such a feature of our human lives did away with the need for further examination or assessment.

In truth, it must also be said that patients of fertility clinics are often failed by the Church also. Arguments over the status of embryos, for example, while important, can have the effect of communicating suspicion and a questioning of whether what they are doing is morally defensible. This is unfortunate since what they say about their struggles and frustrations is of import- ance to all of us.

In general, in the Church we are guilty of taking our eye off the ball. We currently divert ourselves with squabbles over which intimate relationships are acceptable, as in the case of homosexuality. At the same time we forgo the chance to tell the world why it is that relationships are important at all.

The End of Life

Diane Pretty wished to claim a 'right to die'. This is not the place to rehearse the arguments against allowing euthanasia, except tangentially. Our concern will rather be to draw attention to the drawbacks of such autonomy-based ways of framing the ques- tion about how to treat those close to death.

The right to die is an odd sort of a right to claim. First, there is the question of whether we can ever be said to have the capacity to choose death. Death (even for a religious believer) is an imponderable. It is simply not something that we can put in the scales of deliberation.

Second, rights generally protect our autonomy over what happens in our lives. A right to die takes us over this boundary, into an area in which autonomy no longer exists. A related point is made by John Stuart Mill when he asserts that people should not be allowed voluntarily to sell themselves into slavery.[16] What is being questioned is whether we can take an autonomous decision to end our autonomy.

Third, a right to die is a very odd sort of right in that it runs contrary to very deeply embedded moral instincts and conflicts with our actual behaviour when faced with people who might be seen as exercising such a right. Doctors who receive attempted suicides at the A&E Department do not enquire as to their competence to make such decisions, but simply act to save the person's life first and ask questions afterwards. In the context of higher education, as in many other communities, suicide is never treated as a matter of personal choice. Everyone involved in the life of a college knows what a disaster a student suicide is. When such things happen, what no one says is 'Well, that was their decision and we must respect it.' The anger, the hurt and the distress all point to the opposite conclusion, that for all our talk of rights and personal autonomy, someone who does kill themselves is doing something that is simply bad.

It is for that reason that I say that consideration of the right to die shows up some of the drawbacks of the language of rights. Such language obscures what is at issue, which is that of objective goods and objective harms and what they are. The exercise of autonomy is only half the question, because even the most enthusiastic exponent of a rights-based approach to morality would not claim that personal autonomy should be unfettered. We can only have the right to do what we want so long as it does not harm others This harm principle is the key to most discussions. What sorts of harm are acceptable and what sorts are not? That discussion immediately takes us into considerations of substantive goods and away from merely allowing people to choose what they want. In the case of our reaction to suicide, it seems that we consider that the harm involved spreads more widely than the person who kills themself.

So the argument about imposing one's views on others cuts both ways. *Any* policy with regard to euthanasia will embody a view of the good in regard to dying, and so any policy will represent the imposing of one group's views on others.

So a more fruitful recasting of what is at issue in the debate over euthanasia would move our attention away from whether we have a right to die, and towards the question of what constitutes a good death (which after all is closer to the Greek root of the word, *eu- thanatos*, meaning a good or easy death). Those in favour of euthanasia will speak of the dignity of making one's own decisions. Those who oppose euthanasia will point to the value in caring for the seriously ill, of not abandoning them in their distress, and to the possibilities of palliative care that are opened up if we don't go down the route to euthanasia. They will emphasize the way that such caring is an important part of the network of relationships that sustain us as human beings. The language of a right to die simply serves to shut off that discussion.

A fundamental problem with addressing questions about how to treat patients whose death is close is precisely that the autonomy that talk of rights presupposes is absent, often terminally so. Thus particular problems are raised by patients in a persistent vegetative state (PVS). However, the basis upon which they are resolved is not that such people are dead already and therefore have no moral status.

The most widely discussed case is that of Tony Bland, who died after lengthy consideration of his case in the courts in 1993.[17] The House of Lords eventually decided that it would be lawful to withdraw tube feeding because such intervention did not promote Tony Bland's best interests. This decision continues to raise difficult moral questions, but what is significant to note here is that it was not reached on the basis that Tony Bland had ceased to matter. However, a sentience-based view would suggest that this should have been the case.

No one suggested, for example, that because Tony Bland had irretrievably lost consciousness it would be acceptable to take his body and dispose of it, or, for that matter, to do any of the other things that one does with dead bodies, such as conduct a post-mortem examination, or dissect it for purposes of medical education. In the latter case a breathing body would presumably be of more educational value to medical students than a preserved one. Nor is it merely out of respect for the feelings of the carers or relatives that such courses of action are ruled out. Such things, if done, would be wrongs done to Tony Bland, unconscious though he was, and not just harms to the tender feelings of his nurses or family members.

The argument can be pressed further, beyond even the point of death. The medical profession has been rocked in recent years by the scandals, particularly at Bristol and Alder Hey, over the retention of children's organs after they have died. Parents have been distressed to discover that parts, sometimes significant parts, of their children's bodies were retained in the hospital after a post-mortem examination. Who had been wronged by this? The children concerned were clearly unaware of what had happened, since they were dead by the time the alleged wrong was done. However, the parents did not feel that this was something that had been done *to them*, the ones who felt the distress. They felt rather that this was something that had been *done to their dead children*, and that they felt distressed on their children's behalf.

The drawbacks of an approach that sees only sentience as mattering morally are clear. The moral space that people occupy is larger than their conscious experience. Any rights-based approach, concentrating on either autonomy or sentience, will overlook or downgrade those parts of our lives where these are absent, or present only in an impaired form.

Even in secular terms such a constraint does not make sense. Large numbers of environmental philosophers, and in particular the proponents of 'deep ecology', are impatient of such a view. How are we to account for the value of whole species, of ecosystems or of landscapes, if it all has to be funnelled through the consciousness of some being, human or animal? Isn't it simpler to say that such things matter for reasons other than the consciousness that they contain? An approach that sees us most fundamentally not as isolated individuals defined by the exercise of our will, but as *creatures* and part of a creation that is wider and more variegated than can ever be captured by our understanding of it, is much more able to accommodate such insights. Thus it is not at all odd that we feel that when caring for individuals who are suffering or who have been harmed in some way, that our duties towards them do not *decrease* as their capacities grow less, but actually the reverse. The more vulnerable, the more ill they are (particularly the very old or the very young), the *stronger* we feel are our obligations towards them. The Christian account of why this is so is rooted in our creaturely nature, and in the reverence we owe to other parts of the creation and others made in the image of the creator.

Conclusion

We can see in these examples the way in which the language of rights captures only part of the ethical debate over issues of life and death, and by extension any issue that affects humans deeply. In each case the debate can be seen to draw on the richer ('thicker' or more culturally conditioned) resources that are on offer in the Christian tradition.

When we consider infertility treatment and the use of IVF, we can see that accounts of the significance of our having of children that see it only in terms of choices fail to grasp the covenantal aspect to many significant human relationships. Behind the rhetoric of rights society continues to live off the accumulated capital of Christian practice and thought in this area.

In the case of Diane Pretty the courts drew back from recognizing a right to die, despite the fact that the unfettered application of the logic of choice would suggest the reverse. It is submitted here that such a (welcome) reluctance draws on a deeper and unarticulated regard for human life as something that is larger than the view we have of it, or the feelings we have about it. In religious terms this is rooted in a view of the world as created and not just as an accidental, brute given.

Reverence for life as such and respect for the dignity of humanity is, of course, also appealed to by secular human rights theorists. However, something more is needed if such appeals are to move beyond the level of mere assertion. As in the case of the desire to have children, the givenness of such feelings, while acknowledged and welcomed, requires something more to be said about them. It is the Church's contribution to offer an account of what that more might be.

In principle, such resources should be offered by a variety of different traditions. In practice it seems that it is only the religious ones that do, and in this regard the Christian tradition still, in the West at least, plays the leading role for historical reasons. This will continue to be the case, for a time at least, almost regardless of whether the Church as an institution flourishes or falters. Within that process there will be a particular role for a church that is established, even in the attenuated form described by Jeremy Morris elsewhere in this volume. Ben Quash talks of the Anglican vocation to presence. The presence of the Anglican Church in parishes and in institutions such as hospitals and universities places it in an important position to facilitate the ethical conversations that are required. In being present to those wrestling with the weighty questions of living and dying that are thrown up by the changing face of medicine, we offer the resources of our tradition. Others will bring their own very necessary contributions. Medical ethics needs the Church. Medical ethics here and now needs the Anglican Church. We assert these needs, however, in a context in which we acknowledge that we all need one another.

Notes

1 BBC News, 23 August 2002, http://news.bbc.co.uk/1/hi/england/2212963.stm.
2 Most immediately there springs to mind the contributions of Dr Jonathan Sacks the Chief Rabbi, drawing on Jewish resources to address shared contemporary problems, most recently in Sacks (2002).
3 Banner (1999).
4 Hauerwas (1986).
5 Hauerwas (1986), p. 81.
6 MacIntyre (1981).
7 There are, of course, more positive accounts of rights offered by others. See, for example, Sagovsky (2002).
8 E.g. Feinberg (1980).
9 Steinbock (1992).
10 See, for example, Chapter 7 of Singer (1993). For a robust critique of consequentialism and of Singer in particular, see Oderberg (2000a and b).
11 Singer in Jamieson (1999), p. 297, emphasis added.
12 In *St George's Healthcare Trust v S* [1998] All ER 673, for example, the Court of Appeal overturned a decision allowing a caesarean section to be performed against her will on a woman who was 36 weeks pregnant and suffering from pre-eclampsia, despite the fact that without the operation there was a large probability that both the mother and baby would have died.
13 E.g. Harris (1998), Pence (2000).
14 O'Neill (2002), Chapter 3.
15 Genesis 17.1–2 (NRSV).
16 Mill (1859), Chapter 5.

17 For a fuller discussion of the Bland case, see Keown (2002), Chapter 19.

References

Banner, M. (1999) 'Turning the world upside down – and some other tasks for dogmatic Christian ethics', in M. Banner, *Christian Ethics and Contemporary Moral Problems*. Cambridge: Cambridge University Press.

Feinberg, J. (1980) 'The rights of animals and unborn generations', in J. Feinberg, *Rights, Justice and the Bounds of Liberty: Essays in Social Philosophy*. Princeton, NJ: Princeton University Press.

Harris, J. (1998) *Clones, Genes and Immortality: Ethics and the Genetic Revolution*. Oxford: Oxford University Press.

Hauerwas, S. (1986) 'Salvation and health: why medicine needs the Church', in S. Hauerwas, *Suffering Presence: Theological Reflections on Medicine, the Mentally Handicapped, and the Church*. Edinburgh: T. & T. Clark.

Jamieson, D. (ed.) (1999) *Singer and His Critics*. Oxford: Blackwell.

Keown, J. (2002) *Euthanasia, Ethics and Public Policy: An Argument Against Legalisation*. Cambridge: Cambridge University Press.

MacIntyre, A. (1981) *After Virtue: A Study in Moral Theory*. London: Duckworth.

Mill, J. S. ([1859] 1989) *On Liberty and Other Writings* (ed. S. Collini). Cambridge: Cambridge University Press.

Oderberg, D. (2000a) *Moral Theory: A Non-Consequentialist Approach*. Oxford: Blackwell.

Oderberg, D. (2000b) *Applied Ethics: A Non-Consequentialist Approach*. Oxford: Blackwell.

O'Neill, O. (2002) *Autonomy and Trust in Bioethics*. Cambridge: Cambridge University Press.

Pence, G. (2000) *Re-Creating Medicine: Ethical Issues at the Frontiers of Medicine*. Lanham, MD: Rowman and Littlefield.

Sacks, J. (2002) *The Dignity of Difference: How to Avoid the Clash of Civilizations*. London: Continuum.

Sagovsky, N. (2002) 'Human rights, divine justice and the churches', in M. Hill (ed.), *Religious Liberty and Human Rights*. Cardiff: University of Wales Press.

Singer, P. (1993), *Practical Ethics* (2nd edn). Cambridge: Cambridge University Press.

Steinbock, B. (1992) *Life Before Birth: The Moral and Legal Status of Embryos and Fetuses*. New York: Oxford University Press.

6

'Come Live with Me and Be My Love': Marriage, Cohabitation and the Church

Duncan Dormor

Since the 1960s there has been a significant, even revolutionary shift in sexual, marital and procreative behaviour and attitudes within Britain[1] with the evolution of a mass divorce culture, the postponement of marriage and childbearing, as well as increasing numbers of people entering marriage after a significant period of cohabitation. Three key developments lie at the heart of this transformation: (1) the (almost) complete separation of sexuality from procreation; (2) a significant renegotiation of the relationship between the sexes; and (3) a shift in moral authority and autonomy from traditional and external sources (State, Church) to the individual. The result has been to transform the couple relationship, which may also be a legal marriage, from a community of need premised upon a clear-cut division of labour between the sexes into a permanent 'do-it-yourself' project privileging the emotional and interpersonal aspects of the relationship. That which might be described as the 'normal biography', the characteristic pattern throughout the life course of men and women, has then been completely rewritten over the course of two generations in ways that have been disorientating and destructive of family life yet have simultaneously been experienced by many as liberating. One prominent aspect of the emergent biography for young people is that 'living together' has replaced courtship or 'going steady' as the chapter characteristically preceding the one headed 'marriage'.

For Christian commentators such rapid change is frequently read as part of a broader narrative of secularization, with the 'end of marriage' seen, or feared to be, a horizon coterminous with the 'end of religion'. The connection between these two domains, that of the intimate man–woman relationship and of religion, is not merely analogous, for as a number of sociologists from quite divergent perspectives have argued, there are significant theoretical and empirical connections.[2] Callum Brown, for example, in his recent controversial contribution to the secularization debate, has made an interesting case for the centrality of changing gender roles in an explanation of the death of Christian culture since the 1950s.[3]

This chapter will focus on contemporary marriage formation and particularly the practice of cohabitation amongst young adults, predominantly aged between 25 and 35, and the Church's attitude towards such couples. I will argue that the rapid escalation in cohabitation of the last two decades does not constitute a fundamental loss of belief in the possibilities inherent in the marriage relationship, as is so often imagined. Indeed, contemporary hopes and expectations of the couple relationship have rarely been greater which is, of course, ironically, a major contributory factor to relationship dissolution.

In making this the focus of what follows, I would like to suggest that it is crucial for the Church to be engaged in a real dialogue with young adults at the outset of their 'relationship careers', in addition to the more traditional pursuits that preoccupy bishops and synods, like the (re)marriage of divorcees within their premises. In what follows, then, I shall give a brief account of marriage and its initiation within the Christian tradition, before proceeding to argue that there has been an historic shift in the couple relationship since the 1960s, the nature (and perhaps inevitability) of which the Church has not fully comprehended. I will then consider the fluid, even chaotic,

climate within which relationships are formed and one prominent stream of sociological interpretation of it, before finally
suggesting that the Church might boldly reformulate its central
claims about the lifelong commitment that is marriage, in ways
that fully recognize the post-patriarchal society in which we live,
and which involves an abandonment of an undiscriminating
opposition to pre-marital sexual expression and cohabitation.

An Everyday 'Means of Grace'

Unlike the sacraments of baptism or holy communion, Christians have seen marriage in a wider perspective as rooted in the
human pairbond; as a 'gift of God in creation' or as the *Book of
Common Prayer* has it: 'an honourable estate, instituted of God
in the time of man's innocency'. Marriage may be 'adorned by
Christ' through his presence at the wedding in Cana of Galilee,
its nature may be understood in light of Christ's words, for
example, those concerning divorce, or it may be deepened by
theological accounts such as that of Saint Augustine. Yet it
remains the case that there is not, in any fundamental sense,
something called 'Christian marriage'; rather marriage is 'a
reality secular by origin which has acquired a deeper meaning'.[4]
Before turning to the Bible, to Christ or to the Church's authority, Christians make an *a priori* claim for marriage as in some
sense a natural and a universal social institution. In so doing they
are of course in the good company of many philosophical and
religious traditions and individuals, including Aristotle.[5] Furthermore, despite the enthusiasm with which some have picked
over the empirical data yielded by the human sciences, there is
strong evidence to support this central assertion. The social
anthropologist Jack Goody, possibly the greatest contemporary
authority on comparative kinship and marriage, in arguing
against those who suggest that Europe or capitalism 'invented'

childhood, affection between partners or mourning behaviour, states that 'The care of children within a conjugal relationship which is defined by relatively exclusive sexual and marital rights is a quasi-universal.'[6] In short, then, marriage does not 'belong' to Christians and fundamentally there is no theology of Christian marriage, only a Christian theology of marriage[7] which strives to furnish an account of the man–woman relationship that promotes human flourishing.

The heart of the 'institution' under threat is then the reality of the human pairbond, encapsulated in Christian terminology in the idea of the 'one flesh'; the ideal, and the real possibility of a permanent, sexually exclusive and harmonious relationship between a man and woman within which children are reared, nurtured and loved. How that relationship is formed and the ways in which society acknowledges or authorizes such a relationship are important, but secondary issues.

For the early Christians the answers to these questions came with the marriage customs, laws and practices which they inherited primarily, but not exclusively, from the milieu of Greco-Roman culture and from their Jewish background. Members of the early Church simply married 'like everyone else'. Marriage was a secular reality celebrated in a domestic context. What distinguished its nature for believers was simply that it took place between baptized people; what distinguished its character was that such marriages were conducted 'in a Christian spirit'. That is, the primary differences lay with a distinctive ethical conduct; the Church placed particular stress on sexual fidelity amongst men, unlike their contemporaries, and took a harder line on divorce than either Jewish or Roman society, and with what might be described as a marital spirituality; the theological analogy

Christ : Church :: Husband : Wife

with the admonition to men that they should 'love their wives as they do their own bodies',[8] is inherently problematic for us today on account of its patriarchalism, yet within its own terms it presents a very 'high' standard for marital life.

In terms of how marriages were initiated, it is almost certain that a diversity of marriage practice existed in the early Christian communities, reflecting local customs and understanding, a diversity that has led to distinct differences in marriage discipline and liturgy between the traditions of the Orthodox East and the Latin West. While there has been a good deal of fluidity in marriage practices throughout the Christian period, a gradual and definitive shift took place within the first millennium as the secular and domestic emphasis gave way to the sacred and ecclesial with the growing power and influence of the Church from the early Middle Ages. Increasingly extensive jurisdiction generated a pressing need to define when a marriage existed, and as importantly when it did not, primarily so that legal conflicts over property and inheritance could be resolved. At the heart of debate lay a tension between the bequests of the 'will' and the 'flesh', that is between the emphasis on consent within Roman law and upon sexual consummation within Judaism and the Scriptures. Over time, the exchange of mutual consent which took place at the point of betrothal became established as the dominant church understanding of what created the state of marriage. That becoming married was, however, a process rather than an event remained axiomatic, as Philip Reynolds, argues in his summary of the situation in the Middle Ages:

> Getting married was a process rather than a simple act. The spouses initiated their marriage by their betrothal and they consummated it by sexual intercourse. Other elements, such as customs of courtship and the nuptial liturgy, might occur at various points between these terms or before the

betrothal. The state of the partners after their betrothal but before they began to live together or before they consummated their marriage was intermediate and in some respects uncertain, for they were neither single nor married.[9]

As the principle of consent derived from Roman law became more firmly enshrined in canon law, there was an increased focus on the marriage service itself, not primarily as the occasion upon which a couple were blessed, but at which consent was exchanged. Bolstered by the institutional endorsement of marriage as a sacrament,[10] this process culminated in the decision of the Roman Catholic Church at the Council of Trent (1563) that a marriage was only truly valid in the eyes of the Church if it took place in front of a priest in a wedding ceremony. For the churches of the Reformation, however, the primary understanding remained that marriages were formed by the exchange of mutual consent ratified by sexual consummation.

From the sixteenth to eighteenth centuries in Britain a clear understanding that mutual consent made a marriage lay at the heart of a plurality of informal marriage customs which reflected or represented a range of different interests (property, kinship, etc.) and local communities.[11] However, such consent did not necessarily translate into permanence: the state of being betrothed, characteristically a yearlong phase in early modern England, could in fact be dissolved within the first year by either party, unless the woman became pregnant.[12] Such widespread acceptance of sexual intimacy prior to a permanent commitment constituted a significant cultural evolution from the practice of earlier centuries and should probably be seen as part of a wider transformation within the early modern period in which deference and patriarchy increasingly gave way to a greater sense of individual autonomy and personal freedom.

The affections and will of the couple progressively displaced the establishment of alliances between families and the transmission of inheritance as the key factor in a decision for marriage.

Concern over the transmission of inheritance was the main impetus behind the Hardwicke Act of 1753 which introduced the public registration of marriage.[13] This legislation, the main effect of which was to extend the power of the State over the individual, marked a watershed in marriage formation and established, in its long wake, what might be termed the 'ceremonial theory of marriage'; that is that marriages are 'made' rather than solemnized by a half-hour religious service on a Saturday afternoon.

This modern *de facto* understanding of marriage as formed by a 'short liturgical burst' which is also a legal event, is then a fairly recent one; and as Kenneth Stevenson[14] has cogently argued, a complete Christian understanding of the most significant day in many people's lives is hardly exhausted by such treatment of marriage as a single quasi-magical legal event. Nor, indeed, does it correspond to the basic human socio-psychological needs that we have, as embodied rational creatures, for time and space in coming to terms with a new social reality.[15] Yet despite being a fairly recent and historically atypical understanding, for the majority of people what the Church has to say about marriage is communicated by, and often limited to, such 'liturgical bursts'. That this stands in sharp contrast with the weight of Christian tradition can be illustrated by a passage from Augustine's *De Bono Conjugali* (On the Good of Marriage), the most influential theological text on marriage within the Catholic West. In considering what the minimum requirements might be for a relationship to constitute a marriage, Augustine states:

It is often asked whether this situation should be called a

marriage: when a man and a woman, neither of whom is married to another, have intercourse with each other, not in order to have children, but out of incontinence solely to have sex and yet faithfully pledge not to do this with anyone else. Perhaps it would not be absurd to call this a marriage, if they made this agreement to last until the death of one of them, and if, although they have not come together for the sake of procreation, they at least do not avoid it, either by not wishing to have children or by acting in an evil way to prevent children being born. But if one or both of these conditions are absent, I do not see how we could call this a marriage.[16]

Two differences from our current situation are perhaps striking: Augustine does not share the contemporary Protestant's acceptance of contraception as a moral option, but nor does he accept the modern ceremonial event understanding of marriage. Indeed, except for prudent contraceptive behaviour (which we might well note under the heading of responsible behaviour) many young cohabiting couples would, in the eyes of the austere African, be married.

An Historic Shift

On account of its centrality to society, the shape that the marriage relationship takes at any particular historic period cannot be divorced from that broader social context; subsequently ethical evaluation of the man–woman relationship must be addressed to and read primarily in relation to a particular context. Jesus's opposition to divorce, for example, should be considered, in part, as a stand against the abuse of power by men discarding wives in a patriarchal society.[17] Similarly, the ethical exhortation of the letter to the Ephesians (see above), is addressed to the context of the Roman *familia*, headed by the *paterfamilias*, the oldest male in direct line, who exercised his authority over all members of the household. Such authority put the head of the household in a position of omnipotence: he even possessed *ius vitae necisque*, the right of life and death over the members of the *familia*, and was entitled to dissolve the marriage of his son or daughter if he thought it appropriate, irrespective of their wishes.[18] Women married young, not long after puberty, and were transferred from the authority of their father to that of their husband.

Likewise if we turn to more recent history: the natural 'givenness' of gender roles with a 'bread-winning' husband and a 'home-making' wife, axiomatic to Christian discussion of family life in the 1950s, has deep roots in the emergence of industrial society which required a separation of home and work, alien to the largely rural society that preceded it, and possibly, to increasing numbers of individuals in a post-industrial society.

At the outset of this chapter I suggested that we have, in the last few decades, lived through a revolution in the couple relationship. This is not intended as hyperbole or rhetoric; there has been a profound structural shift in people's behaviour and societal norms, a shift described by social scientists under the heading of the 'second demographic transition', a descriptive account of the chain of developments connecting the sexual, procreative and relationship formation behaviour of men and women over the second half of the twentieth century which possesses a certain autonomous social logic. There are, of course, many aspects to this change and a range of emphases that could be made in describing them. One obvious and important aspect which has had a major impact upon evolving expectations of marriage is the increasing emancipation of women. A second, which is more difficult to define or chart usually falls, and is as often lamented, under the heading of 'increasing individualism', and is clearly linked to a flight from institutional allegiance, whether that be to political parties, community groups or religious bodies.

In considering the formation of marriage and the emergence of cohabitation, it is, however, a third aspect which I wish to dwell on in more detail. Prompted by the emphasis which Augustine places on receptivity to conception as an essential prerequisite for marriage, it is the acceptance of contraception which I believe involves the most radical break with the Christian past. It was in fact back in 1930 at the Lambeth Conference that Anglicans accepted, in principle, the permissibility of contraception, under certain quite prescribed conditions. However, the advent of new contraceptive methods in the 1960s facilitated changing attitudes and practices and has resulted in the unravelling of the threads which had previously tied marriage, childbearing and sexuality together. For the sociologist Peter Berger, the advent of modern contraceptive methods has led to a 'Promethean break' with the past.[19] Likewise in the judgement of ethicist, Lady Helen Oppenheimer: 'it is hard to overestimate the difference that reliable birth control has made'.[20] The churches, however, have not yet assimilated the social and psychological implications that have flowed from the dissemination of efficient contraceptive methods; as a result, they have not worked through the full ethical implications.

In focusing upon the catalytic role of contraception in this historic shift, I am of course turning to the critical, but often undiscussed, decision by a couple to have a child. At the turn of the 1960s that decision was made indirectly and implicitly through a natural conformity to social norms, in a manner of which Saint Augustine could approve: simply by getting married. Today it is a highly conscious and fraught decision agonized over by couples; its prominence reflected back through the narratives of TV dramas aimed at those in their thirties and forties. It remains, however, a decision which is made by couples in the context of planning a future together and one which places everyday economic considerations to the fore. To gain an understanding of this is, I would argue, central to gaining insight into a fuller understanding of the transformation that has occurred in the last few decades.

Beyond the 'Permissive Society': A Sequence of Change

The introduction of the pill and the IUD in the early 1960s had a profound and yet initially subtle impact upon marital sexuality. The task of simply limiting the number of births within a family had been substantially achieved in the first few decades of the twentieth century with the advent of family limitation on a population-wide scale; a silent moral revolution accomplished, in Susan Watkins' memorable phrase, 'with primitive technology and without generals',[21] that is with *coitus interruptus* and in the face of opposition from Church and State. What the new contraceptive innovations brought, through their effectiveness, was a much greater degree of control: contraception could be used for a range of possible goals including the delay of a first birth within marriage, to plan and space children, in addition to the prevention of pre-nuptial pregnancy.

The first important impact of the pill and IUD, in a world in which pre-marital sex was still counter to prevailing mores, was that it permitted people to marry even younger without that being a commitment to starting a family. The first subtle intimations of change being therefore an increase within marriage cohorts of the gap between marriage and first birth – a crucial step weakening the link between marriage and reproduction. For the first time ever in Britain, marriage ceased to be the automatic threshold for fertility, thereby enlarging 'the calculus of conscious choice' into an area hitherto the domain of the 'taken for granted': the assumed. Couples were faced with a new decision: when to interrupt contraceptive practice in order to conceive.

While it is notoriously difficult to measure, there is a reasonable amount of evidence to suggest that a greater proportion of couples engaged in pre-marital sexual experience after the Second World War than before – a development indicative of a widespread receptivity to the contraceptive innovations and the extension of the sphere of personal choice that it ushered in. Nevertheless this increased dramatically through the 1960s.[22] As modern contraception spread to the unmarried, pre-marital pregnancies began to fall, 'shotgun' marriages virtually disappeared and the age of first marriage began to rise. Near-universal pre-marital sexual experience, 'sleeping together', gradually evolved into the practice of 'living together'. This unconventional choice of cohabitation began as a minority practice in the 1970s but spread rapidly throughout the 1980s, such that from the late 1980s those marrying directly become the minority and an increasing proportion of people regarded it as foolhardy not to cohabit. The *British Social Attitudes* survey of 2000 asked 'Is it a good idea for a couple who intend to get married to live together first?' Some 56 per cent of British people interviewed agreed that it was.[23] With the spread of cohabitation, marriage and the transition to parenthood were thus postponed, though people frequently still marry when the decision to become parents is made.[24] Frequently, although less frequently with each year, for the period of pre-marital cohabitation has been increasing steadily over the past decade and more couples choose to postpone legal marriage to a point later in their relationship, often after the birth of children.

The birth of a child is a highly significant psychological juncture in a relationship. Sadly, it is also a well-documented trigger point for the beginnings of relationship disillusionment and breakdown.[25] It is also the point at which the State takes a more active interest in the support of marriage, in recognition of the fact that 'marriage is still the surest foundation for raising children'.[26] A belief which finds strong empirical support, for while there is clear evidence that marital stability is not affected by pre-marital cohabitation,[27] children born to cohabiting parents are twice as likely to experience parental separation as those born within marriage.[28] The 'piece of paper', as the institution of marriage is so often reductively described and derided, does then seem to retain some real social and psychological power within the everyday; yet the relationship between cohabitation and marriage is clearly evolving rapidly, perhaps reflecting the chaotic and fluid ways in which people negotiate contemporary relationships.

Contesting Coupledom: Love in a Chaotic Climate

One of the most influential interpretations of this fluid situation is that of Anthony Giddens. For him, the contraceptive revolution I have described above has brought in its wake a 'final liberation for sexuality, which thence can become wholly a quality of individuals and their transactions with one another'.[29] Having been tied through its procreative function to strong, even coercive, social norms and customs, sexuality has now been set free to be deployed by individuals as they wish – gaining a good deal of *'plasticity'*. Such a development Giddens warmly embraces as a natural part of an emancipatory movement bringing liberation to all, but especially to heterosexual women and gay and lesbian people. For Giddens such a plastic sexuality is integral to a wider 'generic restructuring of intimacy'[30] in which marriage and the attendant romantic love complex have ceased to be *the* frame of reference for men and women. Rather, marriage has been replaced as the defining 'institution' for coupledom by a new social reality – the 'pure relationship':

> A pure relationship ... refers to a situation where a social relation is entered into for its own sake, for what can be derived by each person from a sustained association with another; and which is continued only in so far as it is thought by both parties to deliver enough satisfactions for each individual to stay within it. Love used to be tied to sexuality, for most of the sexually 'normal' population, through marriage; but now the two are connected more and more via the pure relationship.[31]

For its advocates, such a 'new world' involves the displacement of the 'language of obligation and duty' characteristic of an imposed traditional morality informed by Christian belief, by the practices of 'negotiated commitment and mutual responsibility'[32] exercised by individuals. Far from weakening commitment, such relationships are, Jeffery Weeks argues, 'potentially stronger because they are freely chosen' and 'commitments to mutual care, responsibility and respect are at the heart of these elective relationships'.[33] Anticipating some of the criticisms that could be levelled at such relationships, Weeks smuggles the idea of responsibility back into his account through an advocacy of a new civic identity, a new form of belonging – the 'sexual citizen' – who can engage freely and easily in contemporary 'experiments in living', but naturally does so in a responsible fashion.

Clearly what Giddens is seeking to describe, and Weeks to advocate, is an ideal. An ideal which incorporates a number of attractive features. Perhaps the most obvious of these is the absence of hierarchy or coercion, for the 'pure' relationship incorporates a very strong ideology of egalitarianism. It is an elective arrangement within which autonomy is retained and difference welcomed and maintained. Such a relationship is then highly attractive, for example, to those who perceive marriage to be an instrument of the State or indeed as inherently patriarchal; an institution in which women receive a 'raw deal', be it an unfair share of the domestic and childcare duties, less good health or the possibility of domestic violence and rape. Furthermore, no one is forced into or trapped by such a relationship which can be dissolved without many of the costs (social, legal and allegedly emotional) attendant upon more traditional relationships. In short, the 'pure' relationship allows couples to be who they are without the attendant baggage: historic, social and legal, that the 'institution' of marriage might bring in its wake to a couple's relationship.

The 'pure relationship' is intended, by Giddens, to be both a reasonably accurate sociological description of 'where we are', but also a prescriptive account, an achievable, desirable new place that couples might increasingly inhabit.

As a desirable state there are several things that a Christian might find highly problematic about Giddens's account. Most self-evidently, there is the lack of a commitment to permanence within a relationship and the fact that it remains a game only adults can play – it is blind to the needs children have for stability and nurture.[34] At a deeper level, however, 'pure' relationships are entered into and sustained (for as long as they are maintained) only in so far as they meet the needs, desires or current 'life projects' of the individual concerned. In such an account the sexual and emotional dimensions of the relationship are then subservient to the rationality of utilitarian calculus, and the individual is conceived to be, in the heart of their identity, not a citizen, let alone a whole person, but a consumer: an autonomous rational and free agent engaging in a market with other such beings on a clear contractarian basis. In such and similar sociological accounts, love is reduced to the status of a 'mask', its nature revealed as mere illusion, an idea which exists purely for the satisfaction of other ends.

This is a hopelessly impoverished and inadequate account of the human person from the theological viewpoint, which precludes the possibilities for human flourishing that lie at the heart of a Christian conception of marriage and are predicated on mutual vulnerability (see Ben Quash in this volume[35]); but it is also, perhaps ironically, quite insufficient as a sociological account. As Philip Mellor and Chris Shilling have pointed out, the characterization of the 'pure relationship' certainly 'highlights real tendencies in how many contemporary persons are inclined to understand their sexual relationships',[36] which is unsurprising given the dominance of contractarian thought-processes. Yet it takes little account of the pre-contractual foundations of relationships, that is the emotional bonding that occurs when a couple 'fall in love'[37] a process of merging together which is essential for achieving a sense of belonging and for the development of trust in the other. This dissolution of individuality in the formation of a 'society of two' renders to erotic love an inherently transformative and ritual character, naturally generating a personal and social bond; a 'conjugal' structure. Indeed, *contra* Giddens, the German social scientists Ulrich Beck and Elizabeth Beck-Gernstein argue that a paradox lies at the heart of the modern pursuit of love, with the relentless rise of individualism, the desire for merging, for the transcendence of the self is even greater than before: 'modern love seems to promise a chance of being authentic in a world which otherwise runs on pragmatic solutions and convenient lies'.[38]

A further difficulty lies with the 'pure relationship' as a descriptive account, in that it envisages too radical a break with the past and is inattentive to underlying continuities in the man–woman relationship. Let us return to the practice of cohabitation. Within a couple of decades cohabitation has evolved from being a 'deviant' social practice engaged in by a small minority with less conventional and more 'progressive' views (characteristically the educated, urban-dwelling and less religious) to one adopted by the rest of society including the offspring of Anglican bishops and Tory MPs. As cohabitation has become more acceptable there has been an evolution in the meanings attached to the behaviour. The 'innovators' cohabiting in the 1970s often chose to live together from ideological commitment – for them, marriage was tainted with Christianity, State interference or regarded as inherently patriarchal. Acute Christian observers, while they might distance themselves from the last of these accusations, contemplated in cohabitation a subversive alternative to marriage. However, the radical innovators opened up the range of acceptable choices for subsequent peer groups considering their attitudes to sex, relationships and becoming a parent. As a result, a decade or so on there has been a change in the significance of cohabitation with cohabitees seeing the practice as an essential, even a normative path into marriage. As a corollary to this, pre-marital cohabitation tends therefore to be associated with a higher relative risk of divorce than marrying directly when it is a minority practice, and a lower level of divorce once it has become a majority practice.[39]

Today, for the great majority, cohabitation is an integral part of couple formation blurring the previous clear-cut distinctions between 'going steady', engagement and the early years of marriage. This does not make marriage redundant, indeed nearly three-quarters of men and women under 35 who are childless and cohabiting anticipate getting married at some point, and one-third of these have active plans to do so.[40] Despite the undoubted flight from the traditional, only 9 per cent of couples agree with the statement that 'There is no point getting married – it's only a piece of paper', whereas 59 per cent agree with the statement that 'Even though it might not work out for some people, marriage is still the best kind of relationship.'[41] Information gleaned from survey material does not make for the richest of social constructions; nevertheless it is indicative of and consistent with other evidence[42] which is highly suggestive of a surprising degree of continuity with the past. While evolving in character, the ideal of marriage remains immensely important, despite significant changes in the ideas and practices concerned with its initiation. Nevertheless, there is little doubt that mapping the contemporary contours of early coupledom is a hazardous task in such a time of fluidity. Addressing the issues raised from a Christian perspective is even more perilous. It is also an essential task.

The Church's Voice; the Church's Task

In choosing to head this chapter with the poetic line 'Come live with me and be my love', I seek to stress and affirm that it is a union of persons with all their attendant human richness that lies at the heart of the marriage relationship. Too often, in the contemporary Church's engagement with marriage, it is the bureaucratic and the legal which are to the fore, an inevitable result of being an Established Church with Christian ministers doubling up as registrars. Such an emphasis should not be allowed to obscure the celebration and solemnization of the profoundly intimate personal commitment that is marriage.

However, the line in question is fraught with ambiguity. Originally the opening invitation of a piece of courtly pastoralism by Marlowe, *The Passionate Shepherd to his Love*, which circulated widely in polite circles of the seventeenth century, it generated, at least three prominent 'answers'.[43] Of these, the one I wish to evoke is that of John Donne, a satirical response, *The Baite*, which drags the fantasy of courtly love through a literalization of the metaphor that love with its 'silver hook' is a snare, to the riverbank itself and the reality of fishing – involving as it does the cold, the uncomfortable and the act of killing for consumption. The idyll of pastoral love, Donne suggests, can only exist as part of the games courtiers play; the actual experience of everyday marriage is a little more grounded. Likewise contemporary accounts and aspirations for a couple relationship which stress its essential nature as a free association devoid of the institutional aspects attendant upon a sustained emotional bond have to be unmasked for what they so often are: convenient, egotistical and utilitarian.

The Church has a crucial role in assisting couples to acknowledge and ground their loving in a commitment that goes beyond a contract between two individuals,[44] in a way that speaks of the transcendent dimension of the human pairbond, and which also provides a framework for everyday living. This is a massive task in our society in which, despite the historically high rates of marital and relationship breakdown, the aspirations for a lifelong harmonious and intimate union have not been abandoned; rather, there has been an increased idealization of the couple. Relationships then have to be constructed 'against the odds' in a chaotic social world devoid of secure traditions and clear signposts and within which great emphasis and value are placed upon the importance of the individual.

This challenge is usually addressed by the Church through the pastoral 'hook' that the marriage service provides, and the ritual itself can communicate such messages with a surprisingly high degree of effectiveness. However, this engagement on the part of the Church does require people to get married, and to do so in a church. Until comparatively recently the majority of marriages in Britain were initiated in a religious ceremony. Indeed, a decade ago in 1991, 51 per cent of people marrying for the first time did so within a religious context, but by the year 2000 that figure had fallen significantly, to 36 per cent.[45] While such decline is part of a long-standing trend, its acceleration is no doubt due to the 1994 Marriage Act which allowed civil weddings to be conducted at approved venues, often more attractive venues than the average registry office.[46]

The world of weddings is a market, and an increasingly deregulated one. If the Church wishes to retain influence within it, it needs to take a hard look at its structures and the associated restrictions. Getting married is, among other things, an act of celebration; and many couples, hesitant but initially desirous of a Christian ceremony, find the Church's bureaucracy and rules inaccessible and off-putting. The Church needs to act boldly and swiftly in this highly fluid and rapidly changing situation to fight for its 'market share' against the commercial forces that would seek to turn every celebration of marriage into a themed, and expensive, extravaganza. It would be good, if somewhat optimistic, to think that the Church might take serious steps within a decade of the Marriage Act 1994.

Reform of the rules governing marriage within the Anglican parochial system are important, but as I have suggested in this chapter, the Church needs to rethink its approach to cohabitation and marriage. In conclusion, let me briefly suggest two ways in which the Church might seek to restate and reposition itself:

1. Abandon an undiscriminating opposition to pre-marital sexual intercourse.
2. Broaden the focus from the wedding to marriage; from event to process.

Abandon an Undiscriminating Opposition to Pre-marital Sexual Intercourse

The timbre of Church pronouncements in recent years has been defensive and cautious, seeking to address the nation with

149

authoritative, firm and traditional teaching aimed at upholding the 'sanctity of marriage'. Such an approach is not without its dangers, as David Pailin has pointed out:

> the Achilles' heel of attempts to impose views based on cultural and institutional inheritance is the brute stubbornness of what is experienced. Reality is not what we decide that it is; in the end illusions and delusions are exposed for what they are.[47]

This tendency is exemplified by the House of Bishops' recent teaching document *Marriage*.[48] Two assertions within it, in particular, seem at odds with the 'brute stubbornness' of contemporary reality which I have sought to convey above. The first is that 'Sexual intercourse, as an expression of faithful intimacy, properly belongs within marriage *exclusively*' (my emphasis) and the second that pre-marital cohabitation as a 'route of approaching marriage is exposed to uncertainties and tensions and is not to be recommended'.[49]

The Church has, however, quite simply failed in the contemporary context to articulate a rationale for their opposition to intimate sexual expression outside legal marriage. Such a failure reflects, in part, a lack of conviction within the Church itself. Conservative movements like the prominent US 'True Love Waits' campaign have not been seriously advocated, nor do they even find a resonance in Anglican church life. Rather, I would suggest, sexual chastity which places all the moral significance upon an act, the initiation of sexual practice, and has, for example, little or no interest in the character of marital sexuality,[50] should continue to give way as the touchstone of Christian sexual ethics to a conception of sexual integrity, where the emphasis is more firmly person-centred and contextual. If the Church wishes to retain or, indeed re-establish, influence with many of its members, it might admit as much. While it continues with an undiscriminating approach to sexuality against a backdrop of a complete collapse in the plausibility of religiously based prohibitions on pre-marital sexual expression[51] within Western society, it undermines its voice when it rightly speaks out against premature, promiscuous, casual or coercive uses of sexuality.

The teaching document *Marriage*, while it might reassure an older generation of churchgoers, fails to address its main constituency, for it seeks to answer questions that only the most conservative and sectarian within the Church are posing. It is seen then as largely irrelevant to many who might otherwise seek its guidance; and the Church's continued emphasis on the undesirability of sexuality before marriage is perceived as part of a broader institutional fixation upon sexuality. Rather, the Church needs to find ways of affirming and celebrating erotic love, so that what an earlier Anglican report described as the 'polyphony of love' which 'finds expression in the lovers' bodily union',[52] that is a more holistic person-centred account of sexuality, can be seen for what it is – a more attractive and persuasive account than competing instrumental and reductive ones.

Broaden the Focus from the Wedding to Marriage: From Event to Process

The Church's engagement simply cannot be limited to a consideration of the wedding service. The challenge that cohabitation presents is the challenge to recognize and respond to the processual nature of marriage itself. Although some people may drift into cohabiting, in fact living with someone, especially taking out a mortgage with that person, is not a trivial act, but a highly significant (if not absolute) act of commitment.

151

Churches need to explore ways of engaging with that journey into the absolute commitment that the marriage vows entail through a deeper appreciation of its experiential contours. The parallels with the Christian spiritual journey, both its experiential dimensions and its institutional aspects (e.g. baptism, confirmation), are straightforward, extensive and a considerably under-used resource. Similarly, a number of commentators[53] have looked back to the situation in this country before the civil registration of marriage in 1753 and sought to bring life to a processual approach through liturgical structure, suggesting that increased commitment might be expressed through a reinvention of something akin to an act of betrothal – either as a public or a domestic rite.

Such engagement should not, however, be terminated by a marriage service, albeit one re-conceived as an act of celebration and confirmation rather than an initiation. The couple relationship is a fundamental dimension of everyday life, which for many is the primary place where the transcendent is encountered through the love of another, where the formation of moral character occurs, and where far-reaching decisions relating to the conception, nurture and socialization of children, and the nature and rationale of employment (voluntary or paid) are made and reflected upon. This is the arena in which contemporary couples struggle to determine what equality in a relationship might mean; how to achieve a balance between the conflicting demands of being a parent, a partner and a person; how to navigate the transitions of life or the characteristic stages of marriage; how to maintain intimacy over decades of living together; and, indeed, how to approach the task of repairing their relationship when things go wrong. In short, the Church needs to grasp a vocation for the articulation and advocacy of a marital spirituality which encounters the 'brute stubbornness' of married life and seeks to help men and women and children flourish within it.

'Come live with me, and be my love' is an invitation issuing from desire which renders the speaker vulnerable and affirms the beloved – as such, it is rooted and participates in the nature of love which is God. Such an invitation is not issued lightly; indeed, few of us make a more serious request to embrace otherness, with all the unknowable consequences for our own development as persons, in the course of our lives. It is, then, an invitation that the Church should engage with thoroughly if it wishes to assist people to make marriage a project for life, rather than colluding with a secular individualism which trashes the hopes and dreams for successful unions 'betwixt a man and a woman' by confining them to a series of ever changing life-projects.

Notes

1   In Europe more generally and beyond. See Dormor (2001).
2   Most prominently: Giddens (1992). Also: Beck and Beck-Gernstein (1995); Beck-Gernstein (1999); Collins (1992); Mellor (2001); Mellor and Shilling (1997). Mellor, following Collins, draws on the inheritance of Durkheim to argue that the future of love and marriage is intimately tied up with ideas of transcendence and solidarity and, as such remains, irresistibly religious in nature.
3   Brown concludes that: 'the keys to understanding secularization in Britain are the simultaneous de-pietization of femininity and the de-feminization of piety from the 1960s' (2001), p. 192. Brown also reminds us that the historical origins of the romantic novel lie with evangelical literature (ibid., p. 82).
4   Schillebeeckx (1976), p. xxviii.
5   For example, 'The love between husband and wife is evidently a natural feeling, for Nature has made man even more a pairing than a political animal in so far as the family is an older and more fundamental thing than the state ... human beings cohabit not only to get children but to provide whatever is necessary to a fully formed life', from Aristotle (1953), p. 251.
6   Goody (2000), p. 4.

7 Oppenheimer (1990), p. 8.
8 Ephesians 5:28a.
9 Reynolds (1994), p. 315.
10 Although debate raged between the eleventh and thirteenth centuries, marriage was only formally acknowledged as a sacrament in 1439 at the Council of Florence. Pope Gregory X had, however, expressed his belief in the seven sacraments at the Council of Lyons in 1274.
11 Gillis (1985).
12 Ibid., p. 50.
13 The legislation of 1753 was primarily to the advantage of the aristocracy of the eighteenth century and only secondarily for the emergent bureaucratic needs of the nation-state. See Parker (1990).
14 Stevenson (1991). See also Stevenson (1982).
15 For a more extended consideration of the threefold structure of rites of passage commonly identified by anthropologists, see Dormor (2003).
16 *The Good of Marriage* V.5 in Hunter (1992), p. 106.
17 See standard discussions of the Hillel/Shammai debate, for example, Schrage (1988), p. 91f.
18 Lassen (1997), pp. 105–7.
19 Berger (1980), p. 13.
20 Oppenheimer (1990), p. 3.
21 Coale and Watkins (1986), p. 435.
22 Two in three brides marrying in the late 1950s claimed no sexual experience prior to marriage compared with one in four in the early 1970s; see Dunnell (1979).
23 Barlow *et al.* (2001).
24 'Wanting to have/was having/had just had children' was the second most common reason given by couples in 1994/1995 in explanation of their decision to marry after a period of cohabitation. See Haskey (1999).
25 The literature is extensive on this subject. For two reviews, see Belsky (1990) and Sanders *et al.* (1997).
26 Ministerial Group on the Family (1998).
27 That is, a couple who marry directly are as likely to get divorced as a couple who have cohabited beforehand. See Haskey (1999), and Kiernan (1999).
28 Ermisch and Francesconi (2000).
29 Giddens (1992), p. 27.
30 Ibid., p. 58.
31 Ibid., p. 58.

32 Weeks (1999), p. 43.
33 Ibid., p. 43.
34 See Williams (2000) and Davies (2001).
35 See pp. 38–57.
36 Mellor and Shilling (1997), p. 51.
37 The analysis of Mellor and Shilling (1997) is very much in the sociological tradition of Emile Durkheim (1858–1917), 'it is an effervescent eroticism, expressed ritually as a "cult of the dyad", that provides the pre-contractual foundations of modern contractarian sexual relationships' (p. 52).
38 Beck and Beck-Gernstein (1995), pp. 175–6. Indeed, Beck and Beck-Gernstein go further, describing the contemporary quest for coupledom as a 'secular religion', even as compensation for a religious world that is passing. For a similar analysis of modern love, see Beck-Gernstein (1999); Collins (1992); Mellor (2001), and Mellor and Shilling (1997).
39 Contrast, for example, the findings of Haskey (1992) in his analysis of 1980s' GHS data, and the analysis of pre-marital cohabitation in several European countries by Kiernan (1999), based on data collected in 1996; or, indeed, Haskey's later work based on 1994–1995 data in which he concludes, 'the differences in proportions of marriages ending, between marriages with and without pre-marital cohabitation, is no longer statistically significant' (Haskey, 1999), p. 19.
40 British Household Survey (1998): 30 per cent of men and 25 per cent of women plan to marry and a further 46 per cent of men and 46 per cent of women will 'probably get married at some point'. See Matheson and Babb (2002), p. 43.
41 Barlow et al. (2001), p. 38.
42 See, for example, the demographic evidence provided by Haskey (1999) and Kiernan (1999).
43 From Sir Walter Raleigh, John Donne and Cecil. D. Lewis.
44 The inclusion of a declaration by the community within the wedding service of Common Worship liturgy is to be welcomed in this regard.
45 Two-thirds of such are conducted within the Church of England.
46 Haskey (2002).
47 Pailin (2002), p. 72.
48 House of Bishops (1999).
49 Ibid., p. 8 and p. 11. See also note 41.
50 In this regard it is interesting to note that it was not until as recently as 1991 that the House of Lords recognized the possibility of rape within marriage.

51 The situation regarding exclusivity is quite different. 61 per cent of those interviewed in 2000 believed that 'Extramarital sex is "always wrong"', a proportion which has increased slightly over the last two decades. Barlow *et al.* (2001).

52 House of Bishops (1978), p. 33.

53 Including Professor Adrian Thatcher, Canon Anthony Harvey, Bishop Kenneth Stevenson and the Roman Catholic psychiatrist Dr Jack Dominian.

References

Aristotle (1953) *Nichomachean Ethics* (trans. J. A. K. Thomson). London: Penguin Books.

Barlow, A., Duncan, S., James, G. and Park, A. (2001) 'Just a piece of paper? Marriage and cohabitation', in A. Park, J. Curtice, K. Thomson, L. Jarvis and C. Bromley (eds), *British Social Attitudes: The 18th Report*. London: Sage.

Beck, U. and Beck-Gernstein, E. (1995) *The Normal Chaos of Love*. Cambridge: Polity Press.

Beck-Gernstein, E. (1999) 'On the way to a post-familial family – from a community of need to elected affinities', in M. Featherstone (ed.), *Love and Eroticism*. London: Sage.

Belsky, J. (1990) 'Children and marriage', in F. D. Fincham and T. M. Bradbury (eds), *The Psychology of Marriage*. New York: Guilford.

Berger, P. (1980) *The Heretical Imperative: Contemporary Possibilities of Religious Affirmation*. London: Collins.

Brown, C. G. (2001) *The Death of Christian Britain: Understanding Secularization 1800–2000*. London: Routledge.

Coale, A. and Watkins, S. (1986) *The Decline of Fertility in Europe*. Princeton, NJ: Princeton University Press.

Collins, R. (1992) *Sociological Insight: An Introduction to Non-Obvious Sociology* (second edn). Oxford: Oxford University Press.

Davies, J. (2001) 'Welcome to the pied piper', in A. Thatcher (ed.), *Celebrating Christian Marriage*. Edinburgh: T. & T. Clark.

Dormor, D. J. (2001) 'Marriage and the second demographic transition in Europe: a review', in A. Thatcher (ed), *Celebrating Christian Marriage*. Edinburgh: T. & T. Clark.

Dormor, D. J. (forthcoming, 2003) *Just Cohabiting: A Christian Reassessment of Living Together*. London: DLT.

Dunnell, K. (1979) *Family Formation 1976*. OPCS, London: HMSO.

Ermisch, J. and Francesconi, M. (2000) 'Marriage and cohabitation', in R. Berthoud and J. Gershuny (eds), *Seven Years in the Lives of British Families*. Cambridge: Polity Press.

Giddens, A. (1992) *The Transformation of Intimacy: Sexuality, Love and Eroticism in Modern Societies*. Cambridge: Polity Press.

Gillis, J. R. (1985) *For Better, For Worse: British Marriages, 1600 to the Present*. Oxford: Oxford University Press.

Goody, J. (2000) *The European Family: An Historico-Anthropological Essay*. Oxford: Blackwell Publishing.

Haskey, J. (1992) 'Pre-marital cohabitation and the probability of subsequent divorce: analyses using new data from the General Household Survey', *Population Trends*, 68, 10–19.

Haskey, J. (1999) 'Cohabitational and marital histories of adults in Great Britain', *Population Trends*, 96, 13–24.

Haskey, J. (2002) 'Marriages in approved premises and register offices in England and Wales: the proportion of couples who marry away from home', *Population Trends*, 107, 35–52.

House of Bishops (1978) *Marriage and the Church's Task*. London: CIO.

House of Bishops (1999) *Marriage: A Teaching Document of the Church of England*. London: Church House Publishing.

Hunter, D. G. (ed.) (1992) *Marriage in the Early Church*. Minneapolis: Fortress Press.

Kiernan, K. (1999) 'Cohabitation in Western Europe', *Population Trends*, 96, 25–32.

Lassen, E. M. (1997) 'The Roman family: ideal and metaphor', in H. Moxnes (ed.), *Constructing Early Christian Families*. London: Routledge.

Matheson, J. I. and Babb, P. (eds) (2002) *Social Trends*. London: HMSO.

Mellor, P. A. (2001) 'Sacred love: religion, marriage and l'amour fou', in A. Thatcher (ed.), *Celebrating Christian Marriage*. Edinburgh: T. & T. Clark.

Mellor, P. A. and Shilling, C. (1997) 'Confluent love and the cult of the dyad: the pre-contractual foundations of contractarian sexual relationships', in J. Davies and G. Loughlin (eds.), *Sex These Days: Essays on Theology, Sexuality and Society*. Sheffield: Sheffield Academic Press.

Ministerial Group on the Family (1998) *Supporting Families: A Consultation Document*. London: HMSO.

Oppenheimer, H. (1990) *Marriage*. London: Mowbray.

Pailin, D. (2002) 'But who am I? The question of the theologian rather than the question to the theologian', in M. Chapman (ed.), *The Future of Liberal Theology*. Aldershot: Ashgate.

Parker, S. (1990) *Informal Marriage, Cohabitation and the Law, 1760–1989*. Basingstoke: Macmillan.

Reynolds, P. (1994) *Marriage in the Western Church: The Christianization of Marriage during the Patristic and Early Medieval Periods*. Leiden: E. J. Brill.

Sanders, R. M., Nicholson, J. M. and Floyd, F. J. (1997) 'Couples' relationships and children', in W. K. Halford and H. J. Markham (eds), *Clinical Handbook of Marriage and Couple Interventions*. Chichester: Wiley.

Schillebeeckx, E. (1976) *Marriage: Human Reality and Sacred Mystery*. London: Sheed and Ward.

Schrage, W. (1988) *The Ethics of the New Testament*. Edinburgh: T. & T. Clark.

Stevenson, K. (1982) *Nuptial Blessing*. London: SPCK.

Stevenson, K. (1991) 'The marriage service', in M. Perham (ed.) *Liturgy 2000*. London: SPCK.

Weeks, J. (1999) 'The sexual citizen', in M. Featherstone (ed.), *Love and Eroticism*. London: Sage.

Williams, R. (2000) *Lost Icons: Reflections on Cultural Bereavement*. Edinburgh: T. & T. Clark.

Part IV

Identity

7

The Future of Church and State

Jeremy Morris

Introduction

Whatever is Establishment in England *for*? Not Anglicans alone, but many others find themselves asking that question ever more insistently today. Superficially – at least if we are to follow the broadsheets' discussion – the answer seems to be 'not very much'. Local church life, after all, differs little from one tradition to another. Over a century of liturgical renewal has ironed out many of the once striking differences between Anglicans and others in forms of public worship. Church associations and social life are much the same, whatever your denomination. Simply being a Christian by itself marks you out now as different. Being Anglican specifically, or Methodist or Baptist or Roman Catholic no longer defines principally who we are. 'Establishment', on the other hand, appears exotic, residual, archaic or just quaint – bishops in the House of Lords, the Supreme Governorship of the monarch, Parliament's residual ecclesiastical authority, Crown appointments, occasional State services at St Paul's or Westminster Abbey.

Yet, for Anglicans, Establishment still does make a difference. It underwrites marriage law and its procedure, with clergy doubling as civil registrars, and a legal entitlement to marriage in church. Baptisms and funerals are undergirded by historic assumptions derived from the 'national' character of the Church of England. Clergy symbolize – whether they like it or not – pastoral responsibility as comprehensive and indiscriminate, available to the whole community irrespective of belief. Establishment often covertly protects and enhances the parish church as a focal point for grief and for celebration, as, for example, after the deaths of Princess Diana and the Queen Mother, and the Soham murders of August 2002, but also the Golden Jubilee.

You can have Anglicanism without Establishment, of course. Many years ago Austin Farrer set out two markers for his own adherence to the Church of England: 'I dare not dissociate myself from the apostolic ministry, and the continuous sacramental life of the Church ... [and] I dare not profess belief in the great Papal error.'[1] Farrer's two theological boundaries admittedly reflect a High Churchman's view of things, but they do provide a crude rule of thumb for key elements of Anglicanism: the traditional threefold ministry, and provincial autonomy.[2] Farrer takes for granted here the Scriptures, the creeds, and the sacraments, and has almost nothing to say directly about Establishment. The growth of the world-wide Anglican communion has advanced immeasurably the argument that 'Anglicanism' does not depend on any positive support or privilege from the State. Even the English context suggests as much, with Anglicans persecuted under Mary and again under the Commonwealth – though we should be alert to the dangers of reading modern denominational identities back crudely into the sixteenth and seventeenth centuries.

Establishment is a fact, nevertheless – brute to some, blessed to others. Can it be defended? What criticisms might be made of it, and what weight should Anglicans attach to them? In this chapter, I take up a position that I hope is not merely a reflection of my own prejudices, but which tries to assess the direction of change in Church–State relations, and to take a prospective view of them. This is, after all, a volume on the future of the Church of England, and, thinking of Establishment in that light, things do not look particularly rosy.

162

First, though, a closer look is needed at what Establishment actually means today, and that in turn entails a historical review of Church–State relations. Only then can we put in context arguments for and against continuation of the historic link, and assess their contemporary relevance.

A Very Short History of the English Establishment

Establishment, as we know it today, has a specific historical form that is much more recent and itself more 'modern' than is usually assumed. It is quite different, in other words, from Establishment as it was in the sixteenth and seventeenth centuries, conditioned by different legal arrangements and by altogether different assumptions about society, religion and political authority.[3] A survey of its history suggests that the situation of the Church of England today actually is more like one of incomplete disestablishment.

The development of Church–State relations in England can be summarized usefully through three main phases, or paradigms.[4] The first began with the Reformation. The medieval Papal understanding of sovereignty asserted the coincidence of the temporal and spiritual powers under one authority, the Papacy itself. As Innocent III put it bluntly in the twelfth century, 'the moon derives her light from the sun, and is in truth inferior to the sun ... In the same way the royal power derives its dignity from the pontifical authority.'[5] By implication, political stability required religious uniformity, since secular authority subserved ecclesiastical unity. This view was never uniformly accepted, but it triggered in reaction secular rulers' own attempts to control and manage the Church. In England, Henry VIII's repudiation of papal supremacy was achieved by the simple substitution of monarch for pope – the *royal* supremacy. In an act of breathtaking historical revisionism, the Act in Restraint of Appeals in 1533 asserted the unity of the realm of England from time immemorial as an 'empire ... governed by one supreme head and king'.[6] The Act of Supremacy of the following year drove the point home: 'be it enacted by authority of this present Parliament, that the king our sovereign lord ... shall be taken, accepted, and reputed the only supreme head in earth of the Church of England, called *Anglicana Ecclesiana*'.[7]

The first paradigm, then, is that of *Medieval Christendom*. This was a unitary vision of Church and State which lingered on through the vicissitudes of the Reformation in England, in other words, lasting from about 1533 to about 1689, ending with the Act of Toleration. Uniformity of religion was widely held to be of the essence of the Christian State. Church and State were inseparable dimensions of the one dominion, realm, or 'commonwealth'. The full power of so-called 'secular' authority was applied coercively in an attempt to secure uniformity in religion. This was not conceived as the imposition of one section of the community's will on another, as would be the modern reading of it. Rather, its abiding assumption was the unity and coherence of religious truth. Richard Hooker, for example, all too often depicted today as one of the most prominent theorists in a continuous series of defenders of the *principle* of Establishment, in practice was concerned not so much with this principle *per se* (which most of his 'Puritan' opponents themselves accepted), but with the particular *form* of Church order and governance.

With no strict separation of civil and ecclesiastical authority, monarchs could not really be accused of 'interfering' in the affairs of the Church. Persecution of those who dissented from the dominant pattern of settlement did not seem particularly contentious either. Why, then, did this paradigm come to an end? Briefly, it proved impossible to achieve a settlement that commanded sufficient popular consensus on a narrow enough range of views to ensure that religious difference would not be a source of civil instability. Britain's descent into civil war in the seventeenth century was brought about partly by religious conflict. Its final resolution was deferred to 1688, but from 1642 onwards it was apparent that the old assumptions about the unity of Church and State were disappearing. During the Commonwealth, Anglicanism as we know it now (or episcopacy and the *Book of Common Prayer*) was persecuted. Its reinstatement in 1660, followed by the imposition of a new Anglican settlement in 1662, led to the 'great ejection' of over 2,000 Puritan clergy and their people, and the creation of permanent dissenting bodies outside the 'official' Church. Further religious conflict in the reign of James II led, through the 'Glorious Revolution', to a grudging concession to pluralism, the Act of Toleration of 1689.

The Reformation settlement had fallen apart. It gave way to a second 'paradigm', the *Ancien Régime*. According to Jonathan Clark, this period lasted until 1828-29, ending with repeal of the Test and Corporation Acts and with Catholic Emancipation.[8] The Church was still intrinsically necessary to social stability, but the State stopped short of punitively enforcing religious uniformity. Discriminatory legislation – the 'Clarendon Code' which included the Test and Corporation Acts – supported the Church of England, but religious minorities were left alone, subject to legal constraint. To most people there was still just one Church in England: all other religious groups were, essentially, dissenting sects. For much of the period, these sects were small, and politically irrelevant. 'Establishment' now was used conventionally. It indicated *both* the 'regulating and upholding of the constitution and ordinances of the church recognized by the state' *and* 'the conferring *on a particular religious body* [of] the position of state church' – that is, both legal settlement and constitutional privilege.[9]

But this paradigm in turn broke up, as the privileged position of the Church became untenable. Exclusion of dissenters became increasingly difficult as they grew in number and influence. Their criticism of the unreformed character of the British State received added impetus from events in France after 1789. Religious radicalism shaded into political radicalism.[10] The 'Establishment' of the Church of England looked increasingly vulnerable to political pressure. In a concentrated burst of legislative initiative – after intense political conflict – the unreformed Church and State gave way.[11] Repeal of the Test and Corporation Acts in 1828 and Catholic Emancipation in 1829, forced on a reluctant Tory government by crisis in Ireland, destroyed the exclusive access of Anglicans to national politics. Dissenters, Protestant and Catholic alike, as MPs, could legislate on Church business. Parliamentary reform, secured in 1832 after a disastrous rearguard resistance by the bishops, widened the breach. Numerous measures of reform quickly followed, instituting a new, non-denominational approach to governance – the establishment of civil registration of births, deaths and marriages in 1836, for example, and the abolition of tithe in 1838. Church reform also followed. A succession of measures swept away the worst abuses of the old Church, including extreme disparities in clerical income, 'pluralism' (here holding of several clerical offices simultaneously in order to receive their income), and the non-residence of clergy. So far-reaching in their implications were these years, that it is not going too far to call them the 'second reformation' of the Church.

The *Ancien Régime* gave way to the paradigm of *partial disestablishment*. Virtually all of the material privileges of the Church of England were removed. No more grants of State money for church building were ever made after 1824. Church rate (a local church tax) disappeared finally in 1868. In 1871 the ancient universities were finally opened up to non-Anglicans.

The principle of Establishment itself – even in the attenuated form in which it survived in England – was under threat, a fact underlined by the disestablishment of the Irish Church in 1869 and the Welsh Church in 1920. The idea of one Church in England and many sects survived only in the minds of the deluded and the obscurantist; it gave way to the idea of competing denominations.

It is easy to miss something vital in all this. The partial disestablishment of the Church tells us as much about the development of the State as it does about the Church itself. The intensity of sectarian conflict in the nineteenth century persuaded social reformers that social amelioration was to be sought through means outside the agency of the Church. Thus the development of the British State was deliberately and self-consciously non-denominational. In time it became overtly secular. That change was accepted eventually by all main political parties, and consolidated by the progressive democratization of Parliamentary government. One only has to look at the fraught nature of community conflict between Anglicans and Nonconformists over church rate, social welfare and education to see how that was so.[12] Thus if, in the seventeenth century, civil war had been overcome only by a certain measure of religious pluralism, in the nineteenth century sectarian conflict over local welfare, government, education and church was overcome only by the development of a view of political action completely separate from religious belief. England had ceased to be a 'confessional State' in any meaningful or operative sense. By the end of the nineteenth century, as Peter Hinchliff has pointed out, Establishment 'was a confused and incomprehensible thing'.[13]

Awareness of that fact explains why non-Anglicans look askance at contemporary Anglican defence of Establishment. Establishment does not preserve significant influence for the Church at the heart of government. On the contrary, the very

167

development of the British State over the last century and a half has almost taken for granted the Church's *irrelevance* in most areas of policy – the one important exception perhaps being education (and even there the Church's involvement is limited but controverted). Establishment does not preserve Christian truth as an operative principle in government, because the vast majority of our fellow citizens choose for it not to be so. The Nonconformist struggle for the rights of individual conscience constituted perhaps the single most important influence of any religious group on the development of modern British politics. And yet, what was originally a disagreement within Christianity became a disagreement over the relevance of religion in public policy altogether. It set the scene for the occlusion of overt confessional commitment in modern political discourse.[14]

Yet, such as it is, Establishment remains significant for the Church itself, and it maintains some opportunities at least for promoting Christian values. The general irrelevance of the Church to government is not in itself, then, a reason for further disestablishment. Much might be made of the connection as it stands now from the Church's point of view. Hidden benefits, apart from public policy and action, might also accrue to society more generally from the continuing link of Church and State. Might there be, too, a matter of principle to be defended for as long as is possible? What arguments are currently mounted for and against Establishment?

Arguments for and against Establishment

There is a long history to the development of arguments over Establishment, but, as we have seen, for a long time what was under contention was not so much the principle itself, as the shape and content of Establishment. It was only when the principle itself came under serious attack that explicit theoretical defences of it moved into the foreground. Accordingly, the 'classic' period of pro-Establishment theory was that of its greatest threat, the late eighteenth and early nineteenth centuries.[15] At this time, under the influence of Enlightenment criticism and the French Revolution (with its reform and proscription of the Catholic Church), there was a growing and vociferous section of the population who made the case forcefully for the overthrow of the Church–State link.

In reaction, Edmund Burke (1729–97), in his *Reflections on the Revolution in France* (1790), provided what remained for the next 50 years or so the overarching justification for the existing framework of Church–State relations. Burke resisted the radical argument that defects in government and society could be corrected by dismantling ancient institutions and creating new ones in their place. Society was an organism, evolving in time, adjusting to new challenges, and composed of mutually interdependent bodies: Providence was 'a stupendous wisdom' which moulded together 'the great mysterious incorporation of the human race'.[16] The Church – the truth of whose claims Burke did not so much argue as assume – was properly the subject of oversight and protection by the State: 'If you will have religion publicly practised and publicly taught, you must have a power to say what that religion will be which you will protect and encourage.'[17] Thus the State was perfectly entitled to impose subscription to the Thirty-Nine Articles as a condition of holding public office.

Burke's argument was followed in outline by Samuel Taylor Coleridge in his *On the Constitution of Church and State* (1830) and by W.E. Gladstone, in his *The State in its Relations with the Church* (1838). Both, like Burke, assumed that arguments about Church–State relations were actually arguments about society as a whole. Coleridge, though to all intents and purposes a convinced Anglican long before 1830, was concerned not so much

169

with the particular ecclesiological claims of the Church of England, as with the Church's educative role as the source of moral truth and public value. In every parish throughout the kingdom there is 'transplanted a germ of civilization: that in the remotest villages there is a nucleus, round which the capabilities of the place may crystallize and brighten'.[18] This was the 'unobtrusive, continuous agency of a Protestant Church Establishment' which the patriot could not estimate 'at too high a price'. Gladstone took even stronger ground, developing Burke's and Coleridge's thought into an argument for the 'moral personality' of the State, a 'personality' which therefore rightly should possess and exercise a conscience, informed by the Church's apprehension of the truth.[19]

Gladstone's case is a telling one, though. He never abandoned his theory. But, as a practical politician, he realized quickly that it was fast becoming unworkable as a basis for public policy. Member of a cabinet which took the highly controversial step of making a grant to a Roman Catholic seminary at Maynooth in Ireland, his defence of the State's moral and religious personality appeared beside the point. Making a principled resignation, nevertheless he acknowledged the weakness of his position. Other approaches than Gladstone's were open to Anglicans at this time. In a complementary development of Coleridge's theory, F. D. Maurice, for example, highlighted the 'national' character of the Church of England, and the Church's 'natural' location within the tripartite ordering of creation, through Nation, Church and Family.[20] Maurice's theory proved to be highly influential, not least because what it seemed to deny to non-Anglican religious bodies was partly balanced by his elaboration of an ecumenical theory which stressed the comprehensiveness of the national church and affirmed the vital nature of the distinctive religious traditions of other churches. Later followers of Maurice tacitly abandoned his assumption of the providentially given character of the State, and amplified his language of national vocation and ecclesial comprehensiveness.[21]

If the argument constructed broadly by Burke, Coleridge, Gladstone and Maurice enabled Anglicans to continue to defend the national church against its Dissenting critics, nevertheless it did not command universal consent even within the Established Church itself. Its last-ditch representative arguably was Roundell Palmer, First Earl of Selborne, whose *Defence of the Church of England against Disestablishment* (1886) claimed that the reasons for Establishment lay more heavily 'on the side of the State than on that of the Church'.[22] But Selborne's case was already weak by the 1880s, and it was eroded further in the early twentieth century by the triumph of Liberal Nonconformity at the 1906 general election, by the disestablishment of the Church in Wales, and by the gradual decline in churchgoing in the early twentieth century.[23]

I shall return briefly to this 'classic' strand of Establishment apologetic later, because its failure to withstand the progressive development of the British State does not mean it has nothing of value to offer Anglicans today. But it is surely significant that modern apologists for Establishment have mostly shirked making the kind of case that Burke, Coleridge and others made. John Moses, in *A Broad and Living Way* (1995), certainly attempted to provide an argument for Establishment rooted in a particular concept of 'Englishness', drawing on a selective survey of English history. But the modest nature of this argument is revealed in a significant rhetorical question: 'Why do English divines continue to affirm that for the sake of church and state there is something in the fact of establishment which remains *serviceable*?'[24] Moses's main defence is covertly a utilitarian one – the 'usefulness' of the Church to the State, and the corresponding benefits the Church in turn receives. A similar argument has emerged from the pen of Wesley Carr, who has emphasized the benefits of the 'earthed' establishment in particular – that is, the local, comprehensive pastoral engagement of the Church.[25] For Carr, Establishment is better thought of 'as an *applied, and therefore, evolving set of connections* between church and state than as a theory'.[26] This has the merit of taking seriously the conditions under which the Church of England operates. Nevertheless it does imply a retreat from the ground occupied by Burke.

Only Paul Avis in recent years has seriously attempted to return to the older Anglican view, but his *Church, State and Establishment* (2001) illustrates precisely the difficulties of doing so today. For he seeks to construct an ecumenically sensitive argument for Establishment, based on a concept of 'mission-in-unity', that can accommodate the Church of England's main ecumenical partners.[27] Surveying the chequered history of Establishment apologetic, Avis argues for a recovery of 'the lost language' of Church and State.[28] But he fails to demonstrate how that connects intrinsically with Anglican polity and ecclesiology, and has to fall back implicitly, like Carr, on history, existing opportunities, and the like, for an argument in favour of an Established *Anglican* Church. And that of course is difficult for him, given the ecumenical task he has set himself.

In what I have called the 'classic period' of Establishment apologetic, the defence of the Church–State link depended above all on a particular understanding of the nature of society. According to this, there could be no conceivable separation of 'secular' and 'religious', as government exercised authority under God's providential care, public morality reflected Christian ethics, Church government included and was entwined with civil government, and society was ordered according to a presumed (but itself historically specific) vision of the Christian *imperium*. Though it is in the twentieth century above all that we find the word 'Christendom' falling ever more frequently into Christian reflection on society, the word arguably had much more resonance within this older, Anglican tradition. Modern defenders of Establishment have tacitly abandoned this ground, however. They defend Establishment in a much more limited way. It exists as a historical phenomenon and it is too complex to dismantle, it is useful to the Church and also to the State, it can serve as an ancillary witness to the State, and so on. These are not by any means trivial arguments, but they should be seen for what they are – a concession to pragmatism.

For this reason, opponents of Establishment have little difficulty in mounting a principled attack. Criticisms of Establishment from within Anglicanism itself over the past 150 years or so have worked from a much more realistic grasp of the rapidly changing nature of British government. The rapidity with which the initial High Church Toryism of John Keble and Richard Hurrell Froude gave way to their scepticism about the reformed State's ability to 'interfere' in the affairs of the Church is a sharp illustration of this.[29] Following their lead, it was from within Anglo-Catholicism that some of the most stringent criticisms of Establishment were to be mounted. This was not because Anglo-Catholics could not share a similar vision of a Christian society to that of Burke, for example – indeed, his thinking on tradition, on organic change, and on prescription was immensely influential on them – but because they perceived rightly that, to all intents and purposes, it had ceased to be true as the basis on which practical politics operated. It was, then, an illusion to pretend that the Church could carry on as if nothing had changed. This realization was powerfully expressed in the work of J. N. Figgis.[30] Figgis was not definitely an advocate of disestablishment. For him (as for me) that was not the primary issue in Church–State relations, but rather the relative freedom of the Church within a particular set of constitutional and social arrangements. Figgis warned against the development of the 'absolutist State', and argued for a 'pluralist' conception of society, with many corporate agents counteracting the 'doctrine of State omnipotence'.[31]

Figgis's suspicion of the State has gained weight over the years. The Jubilee Group, under the editorial hand of Ken Leech, has produced a modern counterpart. In *Setting the Church of England Free: The Case for Disestablishment* (2001), a series of contributions converge on a principled argument for social justice, treating the State as itself an obstacle to the full implementation of the Christian vision of society. As Chris Rowlands argues, for the Church to be the Church, to fulfil its divine mission, it must not allow itself to become captive to any one secular model of society and government. This is an eschatological objection: while still living in this age, 'the church is bound to have to make choices about the extent of its involvement ... based on its assessment of the extent to which ... the kingdoms of this world manifest the way of the Messiah'.[32] Establishment associates the Church closely with the flawed institution of monarchy, according to Tom Hurcombe, and so the Church of England is 'married to the political status quo'.[33] Its prophetic witness is blunted by this compromise – a point taken up by Valerie Pitt, whose sensitivity to the troubled history of Establishment in England makes for a powerful reading of the current situation. As she argues, the Anglican settlement inevitably assumed and defended key elements of the hierarchical ordering of society – it was 'a political and legal apparatus set up by the Tudor monarchs to ensure that the papal writ did not run in England and Wales, and to control the clergy and, through them, the church'.[34] But this is forgotten in modern defences of Establishment (as I have argued above). Instead reliance is placed on a presumed 'folk religiousness' that actually ceased to exist a long time ago, and that is, Pitt argues, a 'lie', which is 'actually paralysing', since it means that the Church 'does not really know what the people are like and neither does it understand its own identity'.[35]

Now to some extent the case against Establishment here is made out of the distorted historiography of modern secularization, whereby the absence of religious identity and affiliation is assumed as the basal fact (particularly for the working class) of the social history of religion in Britain.[36] Even so, much of the force of the case remains, because it is much less prone to exaggerate the degree of influence the Church of England actually wields in public policy today. It is shorn, in other words, of the temptation to blunt the imperative of the gospel, and to that extent takes seriously the being and vocation of the Church. If, to adapt Peter Hinchliff's phrase, Church–State relations today are indeed a 'one-sided reciprocity', then these modern critics are under no illusions about the side that gives the most and receives the least in return. And as we have seen, most modern Anglican apologetics has tended to place its trust in arguments that are essentially pragmatic or opportunist. Leech and the other contributors persuasively contrast the values and objectives of the Church with those of practical politics. Moreover, what they commend is not a withdrawal from the world, but rather a withdrawal from mechanisms of political control in order to re-engage more forcefully and critically with the ways of the world.

Nevertheless, even a sympathetic reader might want to ask the question, 'What next?' If withdrawal in order to re-engage is the shape of the best case against Establishment, what might re-engagement itself involve? What shape might it take? How might the Church actually work alongside other associations and organs of the community to bring into being the kind of society it envisages? It is notoriously difficult to attach absolute specificity to Christian political and social action. Yet there is an

intrinsic Utopianism about the Christian vision of human belonging. It is rooted in particular practices of love, generosity
and forgiveness, but places the horizon of the ideal human
society beyond the present into a future which will be brought
into being in God's good time. This dictates an inescapable
ambiguity about the presence of Christians in the State, that
cannot be resolved *either* by Establishment *or* by its dissolution.
As Figgis argued, what really concerns us 'is not so much
whether or not a religious body be in the technical sense established, but whether or not it be conceived as possessing any
living power of self-development'.[37] At best, the relationship of
Church and State can only ever be a conditional one, under
which the Church can work alongside and through the institutions of the State only so far as they conform to the Church's
own vision of what its vocation requires to be affirmed. So we
are caught on the horns of a dilemma. The reality of the British
State today is essentially its secularized basis, given the competing claims of the many different communities of belief and value
it contains. The Church of England cannot afford to ignore this.
It cannot continue to delude itself into thinking that modern
political life is, underneath it all, still very much based on
Christian faith. It must, then, listen, respect and attend to those
of other faith commitments and of none. And yet the Church
does claim its own particular apprehension of truth, out of
which it has evolved a tradition of reflection on society that is
sharply critical of a great deal that our fellow citizens accept as
uncontroversial.

Looking to the Future

Out of this survey of arguments over Church–State relations in
England, two observations are pertinent. First, contemporary
support for Establishment lacks confidence in the authenticity

of the Anglican Church's apprehension of the truth, resting its case finally on pragmatism. The Christian Socialist description of the task of the Church, conversely, has got it about right.[38] The Church must mark out for itself the territory or space which it takes it be the goal of its expansive social commitment, and then seek with all its strength to claim that for Christ. But this space is global – universal, or 'Catholic'. It is not enough, in other words, to specify an exclusive salvationism as the heart of a faith that can never speak to the world outside sharply defined boundaries. Salvation through Christ has implications for the whole of humanity. This is a Church-centred way of thinking. Christianity is intrinsically social, it supplies its own account of what 'social' is and means. Christian Socialism was never adequately conceived as something derivative from materialist economics, but was always principally an ecclesiological theory, with ethical implications. We cannot search for an idealized human community, as Christians, apart from the Church. The Church is itself – as the body of Christ – the perspective or Utopia through which we can see human community as it should be.[39] Such a perspective can never be adequately supplied by the State. By implication, if there is not a degree of radical suspicion – out of hope for a better world – that Christians deploy in their dealings with the State, there is something profoundly wrong.

And yet, second, that vision of human community must itself have a sense of real human possibility, and therefore a grasp on actual policy and political conditions, in order to offer any prospect for hope. Real societies exist in time, with definite historical forms to their government, their polity, their social organization. Radical separatism, if it does not dare to think concretely about the kind of State it might envisage – the kind of State it might want to help to bring into being and to be involved with – risks leaving the institutions by which power is exercised rampant and free. The earlier, 'classic' Anglican

177

tradition of reflection on Establishment dared to do just this concrete thinking, out of an admittedly flawed, idealized or dated understanding of the constitution. Its defence of monarchy, aristocracy, limited representation, and exclusion of non-Anglicans from office can be set to one side, and never in any case (in the hands of Burke, Coleridge, Maurice and others) actually ruled out reform. But its readiness to see political institutions as morally and religiously accountable, and its concern to project the whole of human society including political institutions as the field of God's concern, did carry the implication that there may be reasonable grounds – in certain circumstances – for a close association of Church and State.

In the nature of things, these grounds today seem stronger at local level than they are nationally. In specific contexts such as hospitals or colleges, particular neighbourhoods, villages, or even places of work, it is easier to see how the Church of England might begin better to conceive of 'Establishment' as a provisional mark of Christian possibility. Following my dual emphasis on radical criticism and constructive engagement, this would have to be open-eyed, alert that is to the risks of criticism and willing to accept them. But it would suggest that many elements of Establishment as locally conceived could and should remain in place, as least as long as possible. The Church of England can justify these on the grounds that they represent something of an approximation to elements of Christian community only so long as it can claim honestly to be cultivating a spirit of disciplined attention to the practice of building Christian community. That word 'practice' is crucial. It implies open church buildings, welcoming liturgies, sustained public prayer, shelter, truth-speaking, resistance to prejudice, willingness to risk failure and loss, openness to non-believers, firmness in teaching – in short, everything that a complacent State church too easily neglects. In order to recover greater freedom of criticism within the current set of arrangements nationally, much would have to change within the Church itself. That might include dismantling elements of hierarchical status that owe little or nothing to the proper ordering of the Church and everything to the residual presence of assumptions about property and social influence, such as differentials in stipend, differential conditions of employment, and lay patronage.[40]

All this may not shield me from the accusation of a certain Anglican imperialism. It would require a different kind of essay to construct a justification for a specifically *Anglican* approach to history in preference to others. My aim has been rather to provide the underpinning for such a view, asserting the need for clarity, integrity and enthusiasm in the way Anglicans see the vocation of the Church, and on that basis for a conditional, critical engagement with the institutions of political authority. It is a plea for an end to the game of double bluff that seems to characterize Church–State relations at the moment, with politicians and churchpeople for quite different reasons acquiescing silently in the continuation of a relationship over which there are fundamental differences of understanding. Much has been, and must be, conceded to continuing historical change. The growth of other faith communities in Britain, changing ecumenical relationships, the uncertain status of the monarchy, these among others are factors that ought to force a review of Establishment. But, studied closely, Establishment itself is not a monolithic entity for which one can be 'for' or 'against'. The argument really ought first to be about the nature and purpose of the Church, and its vocation – in God's eyes – to model and bring forward the Kingdom of Christ.

Whatever the pros and cons, what will the future bring? It is impossible not to predict today a continuation of the disestablishing trajectory of the last two centuries. But this will probably happen in a piecemeal way, since Establishment is not one

179

'thing' but a congeries of overlapping institutions and relationships. As I write, it looks as if the bishops may all but disappear from a reformed second chamber. The troubles of the monarchy over the last few years, coupled with the Royal Family's apparent success at drawing support from other faith communities, probably make a modification in the relationship of sovereign and church more likely than ever. This could come about indirectly through the abolition of the Act of Succession that excludes Roman Catholics from the throne. It could also come more radically by severe reform of the monarchy or by its abolition altogether. State occasions might gradually cease automatically to be centred on Westminster Abbey and St Paul's Cathedral. In that eventuality, state services might take place, say, at Westminster Cathedral, or at Methodist Central Hall, or rotate between various sites including secular ones such as the Albert Hall. Symbols are powerful things in the collective consciousness of a people, and the disappearance of these long-fixed connections will at first dent the capacity of the Church to cast itself as the historic seat of the nation's conscience – though, as we have seen, its role in that respect has been attenuated or 'hollowed out' over the centuries anyway.

Nationally, then, two paths are open to us. One is to rid ourselves of the residual encumbrance of Establishment. That is the purer way. In some respects it would be an easier way. But it could not easily escape the charge of retreat and retrenchment. We can say brave words about the value of freedom, but we have to be prepared to accept freedom's cost, not the least of which would be the perception of many that this was a hopeless defeat, a consequence of failing appeal. It would be a responsible way, but it would require strenuous efforts after disestablishment to recommit the Church of England to a radical programme of social critique and action – to reconceive, in other words, its social purpose.

The other way would be to hold on to the wreckage of Establishment for as long as we may. But this way too has its disadvantages. Simply clinging on for the sake of preserving influence will not solve anything. It is not a theologically responsible conception of the Church to see it as dependent on residual functions. It was a jibe against the restored French court after the fall of Napoleon that it had learnt nothing and forgotten nothing. Anglican defences of the *status quo* all too often have that fatal ring about them. Continuation of Establishment, if it is to be defended at all, requires of us as Anglicans a heavy price – a demand not only that we suffer political exposure and politicians' interference, but that we have a redoubled determination to resist the encroachment of privilege, pride and influence. Are we really prepared to pay that price? We had better be.

Notes

1 Farrer (1973), p. 50.
2 They do not constitute a *sufficient* definition, of course, as consideration of the Old Catholic, Orthodox and Nordic Lutheran churches suggests.
3 This may be an appropriate moment to point out that the language of Establishment itself has changed markedly in the course of over four hundred years. The word 'Establishment', for reasons that will become apparent, scarcely features in British religious discourse in the period before the eighteenth century, and it is therefore strictly anachronistic to use it as a convenient term for Church–State relations any earlier than that. A similar point can be made about the word 'Anglicanism', which I have used as a term of convenience, but which came into use only in the nineteenth century, and then at first as a party label, denoting Tractarian or High Church views: on this, see Sykes (1995), p. 211. For a survey of changing political terminology which has influenced in part the views expressed in this chapter, see Clark (2000).
4 Anyone interested might want to compare my three paradigms, based on the Church–State relationship, with the three put forward by Paul Avis, which are based on the model of authority

within the Church: the 'Erastian paradigm' (sixteenth and seventeenth centuries), the 'apostolic paradigm' (seventeenth to nineteenth centuries), and the 'baptismal paradigm' (nineteenth century to date). These help to illuminate key changes in a vital element of Anglican ecclesiology, but they blur the equally important question of the Church's relationship to society, that is, its understanding of mission. See Avis (1989), p. xiv.

5   Bettenson (1950), p. 156.
6   Ibid., p. 306.
7   Ibid., p. 319.
8   See especially the first edition of Clark (1985).
9   *Oxford English Dictionary*, 'Establishment'; emphasis added.
10 On the influence of the French Revolution on Britain, see Royle (2000).
11 There is a large and vigorous debate on the causes of this period of unsettlement. One readable guide to its main implications, taking a long view, is Hempton (1996).
12 This is one of most telling lessons of W. R. Ward's examination of local sectarian conflict, in Ward (1972). It is also the main theme of my own study of local religious change: Morris (1992).
13 Hinchliff (1988); Hinchliff's somewhat caustic view of the Establishment can be gleaned from the title of his more extended study of it, Hinchliff (1966).
14 I leave to one side the question of implicit influence, personal motivation, and the impossibility of neutral, objective foundations for politics, all of which would constitute scope for an altogether different form of analysis. My preoccupation here is solely with the commonly accepted basis on which the relations of Church and State stand.
15 I am not suggesting for one moment, of course, that Hooker and others of his age do not have anything of value to contribute to a discussion on the relationship of Church and State.
16 Burke (1790), p. 36.
17 Burke (1772), p. 301.
18 Coleridge (1830), p. 60.
19 Vidler (1945) remains a useful introduction to Gladstone's rather prolix work, particularly because he tries to apply Gladstone's theory to modern (well, 1940s'!) Britain, but it has strictly been overtaken by Butler (1982). All modern study of Gladstone's thought is hugely indebted, however, to Colin Matthew, the editor of Gladstone's diaries: see in particular Matthew (1986), Chapters II, 'Gladstonian Conservatism' and III, 'Church, State, and Free Trade'.
20 See, in particular, Maurice (1838).

182

21 A good example was W. H. Fremantle: see, for example, his Bampton lectures, Fremantle (1885); for an interesting exploration of the implications of this Mauricean perspective for the local church, and for mission, see Nettleship (1982).

22 Selborne (1911), p. 72.

23 Disestablishment in Ireland and Wales gave the lie to the claim that the Established Church could not be maintained on grounds of numbers alone, since the weight of the case in favour of disestablishment in both instances derived from the numerical disproportion between minority Anglicanism and the religious traditions of the majority.

24 Moses (1995), p. 118; emphasis mine.

25 Carr et al. (1999); see also Carr et al. (1992).

26 Carr et al. (1999) p. 8; emphasis mine.

27 Avis (2001), p. 8.

28 Ibid., p. 59.

29 On this, see Rowlands (1989) and also Nockles (1996).

30 On Figgis, see Tucker (1950) and Nicholls (1975).

31 Figgis (1913), p. 50.

32 Rowlands (2001), p. 23.

33 Hurcombe (2001), p. 40.

34 Pitt (2001), pp. 49–50.

35 Pitt (2001) p. 58.

36 For a summary of the state of the argument today, see the 'Introduction' to McLeod (1995). Callum Brown, the most forceful modern critic of secularization theory, pushes 'de-Christianization' in Britain back, effectively, to the 1960s, highlighting in the process the relatively religious character of British industrial and urban society until recent times: see Brown (2001). But even Brown has overstated the recent collapse, and a quite different case can be made from that of the 'residual' argument to describe the state of religious belief and belonging in Britain today, as is done in Jenkins (1999).

37 Figgis (1913), p. 39.

38 Here I pick up, most obviously, on the theological influence of F. D. Maurice, but mediated through the tradition of Charles Gore and William Temple.

39 As F. D. Maurice put it, 'The Church is ... human society in its normal state; the world, that same society irregular and abnormal' (1853), p. 396.

40 It is beyond the scope of this article to construct a theological rationale for Church reform along these lines, though it is hard not bear in mind the common appeal currently to notions of 'servant' and 'collaborative' ministry.

References

Avis, P. D. (1989) *Anglicanism and the Christian Church. Theological Resources in Historical Perspective*. Edinburgh: T. & T. Clark.

Avis, P. D. (2001) *Church, State and Establishment*. London: SPCK.

Bettenson, H. (ed.) (1950) *Documents of the Christian Church*. Oxford: Oxford University Press.

Brown, C. G. (2001) *The Death of Christian Britain*. London: Routledge.

Burke, E. (1772) *Speech on the Acts of Uniformity*, in E. Burke, *Works*. London: Oxford University Press, Vol. III, 1907.

Burke, E. (1790) *Reflections on the Revolution in France*, in E. Burke, *Works*. London: Oxford University Press, Vol. IV, 1907.

Butler, P. (1982) *Gladstone: Church, State and Tractarianism: A Study of his Religious Ideas and Attitudes*. Oxford: Clarendon Press.

Carr, W. *et al.* (1992) *Say One for Me: The Church of England in the Next Decade*. London: SPCK.

Carr, W. *et al.* (1999) 'A developing establishment', *Theology*, CII, 2–10.

Clark, J. C. D. (1985) *English Society 1688–1832: Ideology, Social Structure and Political Practice during the Ancien Régime*. Cambridge: Cambridge University Press.

Clark, J. C. D. (2000) 'Keywords', in J. C. D. Clark, *English Society 1688–1832* (2nd edn). Cambridge: Cambridge University Press.

Coleridge, S. T. (1830) *On the Constitution of Church and State*. London: Dent, 1972.

Farrer, A. M. (1973) 'On being an Anglican', in A. M. Farrar, *The End of Man*. London: SPCK.

Figgis, J. N. (1913) *Churches in the Modern State*. London: Longmans.

Fremantle, W. H. (1885) *The World as the Subject of Redemption*. London: Rivingtons.

Hempton, D. (1996) *Religion and Political Culture in Britain and Ireland: From the Glorious Revolution to the Decline of Empire*. Cambridge: Cambridge University Press.

Hinchliff, P. B. (1966) *The One-sided Reciprocity: A Study in the Modification of the Establishment*. London: DLT.

Hinchliff, P. (1988) 'Church–State relations', in S. W. Sykes and J. E. Booty (eds), *The Study of Anglicanism*. London: SPCK.

Hurcombe, T. (2001) 'Disestablishing the kingdom', in K. Leech (ed.), *Setting the Church of England Free: The Case for Disestablishment*. Croydon: The Jubilee Group.

Jenkins, T. D. (1999) *Religion in English Everyday Life: An Ethnographic Approach*. New York and Oxford: Berghahn Books.

Matthew, H. C. G. (1986) *Gladstone 1809–1874*. Oxford: Clarendon Press.

Maurice, F. D. (1838) *The Kingdom of Christ, or Hints on the Principles, Ordinances, and Constitution of the Catholic Church* (3 vols). London: Darton & Clark.

Maurice, F. D (1853) *Theological Essays*. Cambridge: Macmillan.

McLeod, D. H. (ed.) (1995) *European Religion in the Age of Great Cities 1830–1930*. London: Routledge.

Morris, J. N. (1992) *Religion and Urban Change: Croydon, 1840–1914*. Woodbridge: Boydell & Brewer.

Moses, J. (1995) *A Broad and Living Way: Church and State a Continuing Establishment*. Norwich: Canterbury Press.

Nettleship, L. E. (1982) 'William Fremantle, Samuel Barnett and the broad church origins of Toynbee Hall', *Journal of Ecclesiastical History*, 33: 564–79.

Nicholls, D. (1975) *The Pluralist State*. London: Macmillan.

Nockles, P. B. (1996) 'Church and king: Tractarian politics reappraised', in P. Vaiss (ed.), *From Oxford to the People: Reconsidering Newman and the Oxford Movement*. Leominster: Gracewing.

Pitt, V. (2001) 'The Church by law established', in K. Leech (ed.), *Setting the Church of England Free: The Case for Disestablishment*. Croydon: The Jubilee Group.

Rowlands, C. (2001) 'My kingdom is not of this world', in K. Leech (ed.), *Setting the Church of England Free: The Case for Disestablishment*. Croydon: The Jubilee Group.

Rowlands, J. H. (1989) *Church, State and Society. The Attitudes of John Keble, Richard Hurrell Froude and John Henry Newman, 1827–1845*. Worthing: Churchman.

Royle, E. (2000) *Revolutionary Britannia? Reflections on the Threat of Revolution in Britain, 1789–1848*. Manchester: Manchester University Press.

Selborne, R. P. (1911) *A Defence of the Church of England against Disestablishment* (5th edn). London: Macmillan.

Sykes, S. W. (1995) 'The Genius of Anglicanism', in S. W. Sykes, *Unashamed Anglicanism*. London: DLT.

Tucker, M. G. (1950) *John Neville Figgis: A Study*. London: SPCK.

Vidler, A. (1945) *The Orb and the Cross*. London: SPCK.

Ward, W. R. (1972) *Religion and Society in England 1790–1850*. London: Batsford.

Anglicanism: The Only Answer to Modernity

Timothy Jenkins

Introduction

In order to understand any institution, one needs to grasp the question to which it is a response. By doing so, one can offer a description of its essential components, including its characteristic virtues, modes of working and scale of operation. At the same time, one can avoid the anecdotal analysis of accidental features as if they were symptomatic. My aim is to offer an account of the Anglican vocation in this spirit. This account comes in three parts: first, concerning the setting to which it is a response; second, placing it within the broad context of Christian responses to this setting; and third, considering the specificity of the Anglican solution. My claim is that there is sufficient continuity in the situation that there is enduring sense in the response.

The Problem of Modernity

To begin with, I want to characterize in broad terms the experience of being a Christian believer at this present time. This experience refers less to matters of belief or worship than to the interaction of faith with its context. In other words, I wish to ask to what extent the world seems to confirm or, on the contrary, threatens to deny that faith.

The experience to which I refer operates at three levels. First, at the smallest scale, referring to specific day-by-day experience, parish ministry, for example, or life at the local level in a particular locality, it appears by and large that – from the perspective of a believer – things are going quite well. Aspects of life make sense, the local church makes a difference, individuals come to faith, and people try to live decent lives, and so forth. All believers go on trying to make sense of living faithfully, they have a ministry or a vocation among other things, and there appear to be enough materials in the surrounding world that help them do so. There appears to be a sufficient density of believers for the practices to sustain themselves – even when at quite low levels. That is, there is a worthwhile local engagement, expressed in worship, the development of a common life, and outreach or mission. (This is a useful characterization of the levels of Church life, to which we will return.)

And from within a wider Christian perspective, beyond the confines of the local church, there are always signs of life or forms of intensity of faith, such as lively churches, movements among the young, experiments with worship, and Pentecostalism.

At a second, broader level, however, there is quite a lot of disquiet. The world appears to be full of forces that are indifferent to faith. Whether it is the workings of money, or science's impersonal and relentless questioning, or technology's blind progress, in every case, people feel threatened. This threat is not simply physical, that, say, of ecological disaster, or of eventual war, but because these forces also appear to undermine and diminish the values of human life and faith. This is to such an extent that it may be fair to suggest that impersonal forces, in the form of greed and apathy, self-centredness and lack of discrimination, risk overturning the life of faith. In other words, the believer has a sense that, despite the experience that faith works and provides evidence to the Christian at the small scale of everyday life, on a wider scale there is a potential that the world will undermine or deny the possibility of that faith. There is an unfocused anxiety about what we might call the plausibility of faith, even for believers (or especially for believers).

This anxiety is expressed in the everyday in the way that a great many people, rather than living with any sense of crisis, appear to be able to live without recourse to faith. For these, apathy would be the best description, rather than hostility. And this sense can be expressed within the life of churches, in terms of low levels of commitment and in confusion of aims, in the sapping of energy and morale.

At a third, rather vast and unfocused level, there seems to be, against the second view, a belief in the ultimate goodness of the Universe. People by and large believe, and Christians most earnestly believe, that God made the Universe, and it is good, and it is for us: we are made for salvation, one might say, and salvation is a real possibility. Why people who appear indifferent to the specific claims of the Christian faith nevertheless seem to hold to the benignity of the Cosmos quite as much as do believers might be held to constitute a puzzle. At the moment, however, I am simply concerned to note how widely the broad view is held, including by people who appear to be quite tough-minded.

Now, people in the churches, both leaders and ordinary members, tend to play in and out of these three levels: personal experiences of order and glimpses of worth at a local level; a sense of impersonal forces and the threat of real destruction on a wider level; and a broad belief in Providence, and the ultimate coming-right of things. The elements can be put together in different ways and played off against each other. You can under-play Providence, in a pessimistic fashion, and suggest that the dark forces will probably overwhelm us, or you can suppose optimistically that we shall overcome the risks that beset us. We tend to use our perception and evaluation to back up our advocating a particular course of action.

To sum up, this view of the world has within it a curious sense of potential, both for good and for evil. There is a great uneasiness in it, a tension, that is increased by the double sense that here we have the elements of something very good, but at the same time, the possibility of making the most unutterable mess. We have a sense of the possibility of salvation, but we also fear damnation.

The Birth of the Modern World

What I want to ask, as the next step, is, where does this complex view of the world come from? It is an interesting story. It is, roughly speaking, the history of the modern world, and it contains an account of what the Anglican Church is for.

To put matters crudely, the modern world was born in the sixteenth and seventeenth centuries when the Western Church fell into warring parts. It did so through the notion of freedom, and the right to follow one's own conscience. In the longer perspective, the principal question for human beings has not concerned freedom but how to promote their own flourishing and well-being, and the key to that has been the task of creating order, essentially, a just order. Clearly, one needs elements of freedom, to impose sufficient order that people flourish, but freedom has never been the principal issue. The basic problem has always been not enough order, or the powerful abusing their freedom to exploit the rest. And the great achievement of medieval Christian Europe was to create a settlement in which order, freedom and human flourishing all served each other, at least to a degree.[1] This we call the feudal order, a divine settlement in which justice, power and production work together.

This order fell apart as the Church tried to promote its own interests against those of certain political powers. It insisted upon the right of resistance of believers to secular rulers who opposed its order.[2] In so doing, it created a monster, because the right of resistance was then invoked against the Church, in an outbreak of liberty or freedom taken as a sign of God's Spirit in the world. A period of extraordinary conflict followed. In brief, by promoting its own interests, the Church neglected to promote human flourishing: this is the trauma that lies at the origin of the modern world.

The trio of elements I have described became set against one another: order, in its (Roman) Catholic form, stood against freedom, in its Reformed, Presbyterian embodiment, and human flourishing suffered mightily. Of course, Order has plenty of freedom within it, just as Freedom has in practice – possibly too much – order, and each party claimed that unopposed it was the way to human flourishing, but in practice, Order and Freedom – or superstition and enthusiasm, as Hume[3] has it – horribly blocked each other.

After three generations of religious wars, when, as Montaigne remarks,[4] people acted more cruelly towards one another than had ever been the case in Antiquity or among savages, various leaders decided that peace, human flourishing, was a more pressing and more important demand than religious truth. In France, these leaders were called *les politiques*.[5] People – in Western Europe – had to ask themselves the question of how to promote human flourishing, and they did so very seriously and, one might say, pragmatically. The moves to political science, and to economics, and to how to harness the natural world (and politics, economics and nature were all invented in their modern forms at this time), were undertaken in the knowledge that you cannot simply turn back to the Church and expect it to know best concerning human well-being. One might wish to, but one cannot: that is part of the modern experience.

Here we have some of the main elements of the experience of modernity that I have outlined: various sciences as ways of pursuing well-being, humans come of age, a certain pragmatism (see what will work, rather than being guided by tradition or by 'ultimate questions'), and the failure of religion. All these factors need to be taken seriously.

But there is another element needed to complete the picture. For, of course, just because religion cannot be relied upon does not mean you can turn your back on God. If pragmatism becomes your final horizon, human practices become idolatrous: politics becomes the pursuit of power, economics the seeking of wealth, science the domination of nature – and unintended consequences accumulate in an ever-accelerating fashion. That is no way to promote human flourishing – which was, if you remember, the point of the exercise. And here we have the sense of science, technology, and the market and so forth as a threat – a threat both to our bodies and our souls.

Anglicanism as an Answer

Anglicanism was actually born to meet this situation, and shares the same 'political' spirit. It is first of all a consecration of the political settlement that says order and freedom must both be present, but subordinate to human flourishing. Indeed, Anglicanism contains representative 'parties' favouring order, freedom and human well-being respectively. But the settlement insists that their holding together in a common human project is more important than their independent – and sometimes incompatible – claims to truth.

Second, it is a consecration of the coming of age of the human: it at once supports the world of modernity that was

191

founded, and the human ideal or vocation that underwrites it. And, at the same time, it has the role of recalling these humans to the worship of the one true God, without which all pragmatism becomes idolatry. This is the point of Establishment in the English Church. It is a functional way of continually drawing attention to the need on the part of all responsible people to contest idolatry. What matters is less the form it takes, and more how best to pursue the task.

Anglicanism, in sum, is a facing up of the Christian faith to the failure of religion, and the consequences of taking seriously the continuing project of creating human flourishing under these circumstances. I am only half-joking when I say that Anglicanism is the only answer to modernity.

Christian Responses

Given this account of Anglicanism being well adapted to modernity, what of the other Churches? For Anglicanism is clearly only one settlement among several, and somewhat atypical in the European context. To put matters positively, what life do Christians have in common? What is it that joins them together, beyond the fact that they go to various churches, and therefore might be thought of as species of the genus 'churchgoer'? Do they share any real common life?

The answer to this question includes a historical dimension, as we have seen. In Europe – and beyond – we are indelibly marked by the Reformation, and how the Reformation and its consequences are understood shapes whether one sees any common life to Christians. The commonest position is one that prolongs the contemporary perceptions of that period and which divides the actors in the Reformation into good men and villains: good Christians and not-really Christians. You may call the latter misguided, or foolish, or wicked, or even anti-

Christians, but there is no doubt that there is a distribution of being right and being wrong. It is quite hard, under these circumstances, to envisage any practical common life to Christians in the present. A common life is envisaged in the past, before the Fall/Reformation, or in the future, after repentance for past folly or, most likely, at the Eschaton, but there is never any common life today.

It is possible, however, to offer another view of the Reformation, one that does not divide Christians into the good and the bad. Rather, the Reformation is the fragmentation of the Western Catholic Church, and that the fragments are all true parts of the Body of Christ. Each and every expression of the Christian faith is the work of God in believers: evidence of the ongoing action of Christ for us.

Two things need to be said, one quite complicated, the other quite simple. The complicated thing is this. Just because God is to be found in every Church, this does not mean that every Church is equivalent. From what has been said before, the difference may be put as follows: each Church is a balance of the three elements: order, freedom and human flourishing. They correspond in part to tradition, revelation and reason. The question is, to which do you give priority? The older Churches tend to privilege order as the key to freedom in Christ and to consequent human flourishing. The newer Churches tend to privilege freedom (of conscience) as the key to order and to consequent human flourishing. The Anglican Church, because it was born in the struggle between the advocates of order and those of freedom, tends to suggest that order and freedom should be subservient to human flourishing; in other words, keep your eye on the end, and use the appropriate means. This in fact gives quite another view about how to behave in the world, and what is an appropriate scale for action, and indeed, knowledge. More 'principled' Christian Churches tend to re-gard this pragmatism with suspicion, and sometimes disdain.

But the overall point is all Churches have these three serious theological elements – order, freedom and human flourishing – in play, and they constantly debate their relation, whether in respect to common life, worship or mission. And how they balance them determines many differences. The differences are important, but should be recognized for what they are, differ-ences in balance rather than differences in essence.

This brings us to the second, simple point, which is crucial. If we believe that faith is not owned by the believer, not produced by him or her, but rather is the evidence of God's activity in us, then the faith to be found in every believer, and therefore in every Church, is put into them by God. In which case, to neglect or disparage the faith of others is literally blasphemous: turning our backs upon God's embodied action. In practice, this is a hard saying. But this critique is implied by the Anglican settle-ment, which sees the world as the sphere of God's action, and therefore the faith of others as truly faithful, though not identi-cal to the Anglican vocation. One should not, of course, expect symmetry of recognition between the different Christian settle-ments in such a perspective, nor does it obtain.

The Situation of the Christian Churches

That being so, Anglicanism's vocation is set within this pluralist context; it is one viable response to the modern situation. It is of course a difficult situation, in that it is complex. It is neither a godless world, nor one that is clearly religious. More compli-cated still, the secular world that has been created itself oscillates between demanding order and seeking freedom, each taken on its own as a complete answer to the problem of human well-being. Advocates of authority, order and science, for example,

194

engage in a dialogue of the deaf with promoters of the free market and a morality of individualism. The debates between these total answers generate much of what causes us doubt and even fear. Certainly, they obscure the calling to promote godliness and human flourishing by subordinating both order and liberty to these projects. So it is often difficult to articulate the Christian calling in its specificity, and in general it is something that we do better than talk about, for good reason, for pursuing human flourishing and the worship of God are essentially practices, not theories. But let me try and articulate that calling a little.

From the point of view of Christian people, our vocation will have a number of forces or constraints at work giving it shape. We are called to be Christians, to follow Christ. That call does not go away. Yet, because we are all adult and competent, the church community is divided in its perception of what is important and what its aims are.

Religion is widely distrusted, and its public image in this respect is very different to the believer's experience of it. There are few points of contact between people's personal involvement and commitments with the Christian faith and the public accounts of religion. And yet, on the negative side, there are sufficient examples of abuses of power, acts of idiocy and wickedness attributable to religious people so that it is difficult to make a strong public case for the Church.

The demand for flourishing, or salvation, is, however, widely felt, and pursued by other means, often through institutions that the Church shares in the provision of, relating to schooling, hospitals, care, welfare and charities. We might note that thinking about these institutions is never finished, never perfected, and that the Church may have future as well as past roles to play in these activities. And this is for the following reason; the ever-present threat of idolatry, or the collapse of horizons from the ideal to the pragmatic, and even the self-interested. For the life of institutions continually threatens the projects they carry; this is true of every institution, whether it is the Church, the health service, transport, education of the young, care of the elderly, trade, the provision of food or of energy. In short, modernity has not resolved the problem of sin.

The Anglican Vision

If this description is in any sense valid, how might we set about articulating the Anglican vision? About saying who we are, and why we are, offering a way of articulating a way of living? Note that this articulation has to be done in a certain kind of way. We cannot, for example, simply offer a set of first order principles to define how we should behave, for this is one of the ways of making sense that has been discredited in the fall of religion. Likewise, we cannot claim that the individual lives in a world where he (or she) is free to make sense as best he can. The emphasis upon the priority of human flourishing, and the re-course both to order and to freedom as appropriate to serve that aim, have implications for how one proceeds intellectually, implications – as we shall see – both as to scale and style of engagement.

This account will consider Anglicanism simply within its English context. It is worth remarking that in developing an account of the Anglican vocation, we are led necessarily to narrow the scope to an intermediate scale, situated between global claims and individual needs. This is because of the sort of settlement with which we are concerned. Nevertheless, it is not by that a parochial vision. One of the surprising features of attending international Anglican gatherings is that there are Churches represented from countries outside the sphere of former British rule or influence, Japan, Rwanda, the Congo and

Brazil among them. One reason for the transferable nature of this form of Christianity to places that are or have been troubled in different ways lies, I suggest, in the form of the settlement that Anglicanism represents, a settlement that, if not capable of resolving, is at least capable of holding in tension the antinomies of the modern condition.

I shall approach the task through a set of four questions and answers. First, what does the Church offer this country? Then, what is the basis of the Church's uniqueness? Following that, what is the specificity of the Anglican Church? And finally, what, then, is the role of the Anglican Church? We need not be confined to these four questions, and they are of course extremely general. But they lend us a certain orientation and take us a certain way, giving rise to a number of matters that could be pursued in more detail.

The first question, then, is what does the Church offer this country? We are concerned at this stage with the whole Christian Church. The answer might be, in a suitably Trinitarian formula, three things: first, charity, or the givenness of God; second, the forgiveness of sins, or the way of God in Christ; and third, hope, or the work of the Spirit. Each of these characteristics is clearly capable of extraordinary elaboration, but that is not my point here, which is rather to consider what signs or resources the Church bears for the society of which it is a part. Each of these characteristics, indeed, is borrowed by other, secular institutions, or simulated by them; even 'saying sorry' has had its moment. However, the claim that limitless generosity and true forgiveness and real hope – rather than, say, calculation, repression, and illusion – are the basis of intelligibility and being in this world, is the mark of the Christian Church.

The Church bears witness to the possibility, and more, the reality, of generosity, forgiveness and hope, and that is what the Church is good for, in the eyes of the rest of the social order. Of course, the possibility of charity, redemption and hope are frequently denied in secular discourse, and equally frequently, the Church's adequacy to the task of conveying such possibilities is (often rightly) contested. Nevertheless, if you want to understand the sort of resources the Church offers the country, its particular function or uniqueness, these are the sort of questions to which you will have to look.

So the second question is what is the basis, in practice, of the Church's uniqueness? Here the answer is worship. Worship defines the specificity of the Church's contribution, which might be termed as being ministry in, to and against the society it serves. The Church is organized above all else to provide regular, well-ordered, lively worship, for worship is the life-blood of the Church.

It is true that that the Church should offer a model of community, and that it should pay attention to acts of charity, and that it should join in public reflection upon the way society should be. This is not a plea for the narrowing of the Church's vision and task. But it is to claim that all affirmation, questioning and criticism of the social order is initially perceived and articulated when a common life is offered up, reflected upon and judged through worship and the reading of Scripture in worship. Other sources of affirmation, questioning and criticism need to be taken up and used, but they need to be subjected to criteria that emerge from the business of worship.

Otherwise, the Church simply takes up other discourses, essentially humanistic, pragmatic discourses with their inevitable tendency to idolatry. I have suggested that these discourses tend to take their lowered horizon of expectation, which is to pursue human well-being in a particular context, as an ultimate horizon, and thereby they come to defeat their own purpose. To adopt such an approach is doubly a defeat for the Church, for its task in joining in public discussions is to point to the demands and possibility of God, while at the same time affirming the goodness of the project of promoting the public good, and without making monopolistic (and foolish) claims for the place and importance of the Church. And the Church can only achieve this complex task through regular worship. I will return to this in the last section.

It may be that the millennial task of the Church of England is to make sure that collective daily prayer is going on in all its churches (not Bible studies and quiet times, but regular public worship), and that that will be enough for it to fulfil its calling. It is within its compass to achieve; it has the resources and the buildings. Nobody could object that the Church was straying into territory that is not its own. And the steady supply of (one hopes) increasing numbers of people daily confronted by Scripture and its demands, and ordering their lives around its demands in prayer, would leaven public life in quite unforeseeable ways. So, to repeat, the Church's uniqueness is based upon worship.

The third question that follows is, then, what is the specificity of the Anglican Church? For all that I have said so far applies to all the Christian Churches. As I have already suggested, each Church is defined by its history, by a particular relation to State and people, an ideal model of self-definition and authority, which we might term a political settlement. The Anglican relation to the polity is lived out in two particular and related forms, which respond to the various demands of scale, inclusiveness, human autonomy and style which I have sketched. These two forms may be labelled as 'territorial embeddedness' (which occurs at several levels: parish, diocese and nation) and a 'conversational mode'.

These two forms, in fact, constrain the aspects of Anglican ordained ministry. On the one hand, a priest takes on a territory, and all the people in it, without exception, as his or her responsibility: the cure of souls. This aspect corresponds to the doctrine of the Incarnation: it is the case that God is to be found embodied in a particular place, locality, people; the materials of time and history can show him forth (which is why any ministry is an experiment in Providence, finding out how God is present in a place). And on the other hand, she or he has to engage conversationally, rather than authoritatively, or in an exclusive fashion. This is because no one voice, opinion or understanding can hold an exhaustive account of the glory of God, and only through conversation are our blindnesses remedied. This aspect corresponds to the doctrine of the Mystery of God.

You might remark that these seem to be two negative features of Anglican ministry, or what are often taken to be so: the Anglican Church does not gather like-minded people, nor does it claim a monopoly on the truth. But these characteristics emerge from a positive theology: an understanding of God's working in history as an expression of his character, and a response to it.

We might notice two more things here. These two features – territorial embeddedness and a conversational mode – serve to identify the two characteristic forms of the ministry of the Anglican Church: the gathering of a congregation drawn from a particular place, and what I think of as 'chaplaincy' – being out and about, taking an interest, and 'being used to think with' (in shorthand). This needs to be explored, but it is worth remarking here that much of the Anglican Church's work, at every level (up to the national), is performed in this chaplaincy style: the bishop's public role in the diocese, as much as the priest's around the parish. Note, too, that in a society where, for the moment, fewer people feel licensed or committed or compelled to come to church, 'chaplaincy' will continue to be enormously important to fulfilling the Church's calling. But it must also be said that this work cannot be done without worshipping congregations underwriting it. Both forms are vital, and depend upon each other.

The second thing to note is that such an understanding of the specificity of the Anglican Church (in terms of territory and conversation, congregation and chaplaincy) has a considerable flexibility built in to its relations at different levels with a developing polity. One important feature is that the Anglican Church need not be understood as tied through Establishment to a particular notion of the nation-state, nor need each parish church or diocesan cathedral be seen as a function of that model of polity.

The fourth (and final) question is what, then, is the role or vision for the Anglican Church? Since the Church is embedded and conversational, I cannot tell you in satisfying detail; it has to be worked out on site. But let me say this: the basic issue has not changed since the time of the Venerable Bede (who recorded the Christianization of Britain): the Church has a crucial role to play in the creation and maintenance of a just and peaceful society, so that people may live ordered, quiet and faithful lives. Its concern is human flourishing, which we call salvation, or the Kingdom of God. I acknowledge that one needs to be cautious in making such claims, and that sensible people immediately want to emphasize the eschatological element; that is, to say that the Kingdom of God is not simply human well-being. But I want to make two points by putting things as I do. First, there is a point in concentrating upon human particularities, and not reaching too quickly for the eschatological. Christians need to think against an eschatological horizon, but in a grounded way that might lend some content to the concept. And second, salvation is what the human heart truly desires, and so, the other way about, such things as the human heart truly desires – such as health, and peace, and company, and dying well – have to be comprehended in an account of salvation. Otherwise, once again, we have no content to the concept: it simply trumps human concerns. All that being said, because the issues have not changed, the basic tasks of the Church are the same, even though one must pay attention to the various scales upon which human lives are constructed, and to the constraints created by the recent history described.

In brief, the tasks of the Church are worship, exemplarity or witness, education and call. The congregation's calling is to live and worship locally, welcoming the alien, helping the poor and oppressed, expressing a life in common with other congregations in the place, trying to live out the reality of charity, forgiveness and hope. To this should be added the business of education, both of selves and others, whereby both the principles and practices of flourishing should be explored and transmitted; and the call made to all classes, professions, trades and persons to live up to the height of their calling. All these tasks emphasize the tension between everyday life and the life of the congregation that structures the Anglican vocation.

Intensification and Extension

As a last step, I want to develop a little on two of the topics that have emerged, once again, narrowing the scale. Earlier, I suggested that the life of any church, no matter how small, is focused at three levels – in worship, the development of a common life, and outreach. I want to look in particular at the first and the last: the intensification of worship and the extension of reach, of interest and connection (which is sometimes called mission). These are mediated, of course, by the life of the worshipping community. But if we say that the business of the church is worship, common life and outreach, and we know that the life in all these is the life of God's spirit and not the force of our own wills, then the intensification of worship must be the key to any attempt at development.

The resource for any intensification of faith in our tradition is prayer and reading the Bible, but prayer and reading the Bible have to be put in the context of liturgical worship. This is a complex area; let me try and put things briefly.[6]

First, churches should aim to conduct daily prayer, in a structured form. This is within the compass of most congregations; it demands a small group that feels the call to sustain such a project.

Second, the point of using a liturgy is that it offers a transforming structure. The participants are altered as they pass through it, purged as it were of their own wills and desires, and opened to the mind of God. In this way, their prayers are curiously distanced from their desires, hopes and fears – though not indifferent to them.

Third, this transformation is achieved in large part, I am convinced, by the reading of Scripture in worship. The Bible is the face of God, and in worship, rather than reading the Bible, we are read by it. This business of being read is, again, not a simple matter. We are concerned on the one hand with the way that the Scriptures respond to and converse with one another, being re-read to apply to new situations, most notably, of course, but by no means uniquely, the appearance of the Messiah. And we are concerned on the other hand with reading our own situation analogously with the eyes of faith. This process – of being read by Scripture – is not simple application, but rather the discernment of an always-provisional logic of faith. We are very bad at it, in the contemporary Church; it is a skill that we have to re-learn.

Fourth, and finally, what then occurs in worship is that the participants bring in the world, in their concerns, desires, fears and so forth. They are re-ordered by the complicated business of being read by Scripture in the course of the liturgy, and freed to pray. And these transformed creatures then go out to that world: that world has been subtly changed, because it has been prayed for, and the participants are also subtly changed, a leaven to effect growth and so to continue this dialectic of worship and world.

All that is in shorthand. My claim is that the Bible read in worship is a means of intensification of faith. That to use it so is an extraordinary challenge, because we scarcely know how to do it. But that to do so is within our compass – we have the numbers, and the will, and the means. And, to repeat an earlier point, nobody would deny that that is what the Church is for, whether or not they approve the project.

From this outline, you can see why I believe extension of reach goes hand in hand with this intensification of faith. I will be briefer still on this topic. Learning about the setting of one's faith has to do with what one brings into prayer, but it also has to do with the division of labour. Some will concentrate upon the life of the congregation, and worship, and outreach. Others have principally to take an interest in the place as a whole, make an inventory of institutions, employments, interests and so forth, in short, map out the place in all its dimensions. For example, if you do not know your farmers and the state of the farming industry by the time foot-and-mouth hits, you have left it too late. Both kinds of activity – the congregational and chaplaincy – relate to the other. One gives a content to faith and worship; the other gives a point to knowing about the place. They are complementary forms of ministry; together, they form a matrix which may serve the people, who share the calling to promote human flourishing, but need resources to do so.

In short, engagement with the world and worship of the Christian God cannot be detached from one another. Serious worship of God and being taken seriously by the world are complementary projects, and not opposed. This is our central challenge, and should shape all our thinking about ministry. It seems to me there is no other way of responding to our vocation, if I have perceived it aright: a vocation of affirming a world where man has come of age, where the demand to worship God is as real as it always has been, and where the consequences of idolatry as clear as they ever have been.

Notes

1 See Duby (1980).
2 Figgis (1914).
3 Hume (1777).
4 Montaigne (1580).
5 Toulmin (1990).
6 See Jenkins (2002).

References

Duby, G. (1980) *The Three Orders*. Chicago: University of Chicago Press.

Figgis, J. N. ([1914] 1994) *The Divine Right of Kings*. Bristol: Thoemmes Press.

Hume, D. ([1777] 1992) *Essays*. Oxford: Oxford University Press.

Jenkins, T. (2002) 'An ethical account of ritual: an anthropological description of the Anglican daily office', *Studies in Christian Ethics*, 15: 1–10.

Montaigne, M. ([1580] 1958) 'On cannibals', in M. Montaigne, *Essays*. Harmondsworth: Penguin Books.

Toulmin, S. (1990) *Cosmopolis*. Chicago: University of Chicago Press.